The media's watching Vault!
Here's a sampling of our coverage.

"Unflinching, fly-on-the-wall reports... No one gets past company propaganda to the nitty-gritty inside dope better than these guys."
— *Knight-Ridder newspapers*

"Best way to scope out potential employers...Vault has sharp insight into corporate culture and hiring practices."
— *Yahoo! Internet Life*

"Vault has become a de facto Internet outsourcer of the corporate grapevine."
— *Fortune*

"For those hoping to climb the ladder of success, [Vault's] insights are priceless."
— *Money.com*

"Another killer app for the Internet."
— *The New York Times*

"If only the company profiles on the top sites would list the 'real' information... Sites such as Vault do this, featuring insights and commentary from employees and industry analysts."
— *The Washington Post*

"A rich repository of information about the world of work."
— *Houston Chronicle*

VAULT
> the most trusted name in career information™

VAULT CAREER GUIDE TO
PRIVATE
EQUITY

VAULT CAREER GUIDE TO
PRIVATE EQUITY

MIKE MARTINEZ AND THE STAFF OF VAULT

For information about permission to reproduce selections from this book, contact Vault.com Inc., 150 W. 22nd St., 5th Floor, New York, NY 10011, (212) 366-4212.

Library of Congress CIP Data is available.

ISBN 10: 1-58131-547-3

ISBN 13: 978-1-58131-547-9

Printed in the United States of America

ACKNOWLEDGMENTS

We are extremely grateful to Vault's entire staff for all their help in the editorial, production and marketing processes. Vault also would like to acknowledge the support of our investors, clients, employees, family and friends. Thank you!

Table of Contents

Visit the Vault Finance Career Channel at **www.vault.com/finance**— with
insider firm profiles, message boards, the Vault Finance Job Board and more.

VAULT CAREER LIBRARY   ix

Chapter 8: Private Equity Career Paths 77

FINAL ANALYSIS 83

APPENDIX 85

ABOUT THE AUTHOR 91

Visit the Vault Finance Career Channel at **www.vault.com/finance**— with
insider firm profiles, message boards, the Vault Finance Job Board and more.

VAULT CAREER LIBRARY   xi

Introduction

What is Private Equity?

In its broadest sense, private equity is an investment derived from a nonpublic entity. Of course, under that definition, any individual who owns a single share of stock is, indeed, a private equity investor. The kind of private equity we're talking about is much bigger; these individuals don't just invest in stock—they buy whole companies.

In modern private equity, a pool of capital is created from private investors, ranging from university endowments and pension funds to hedge funds, Wall Street investment banks and high-net-worth individuals. The managers of these private equity pools, or funds, then try to put that capital to work, generally by purchasing private or public companies, "fixing" them so they generate more revenue, cash and earnings, and then "flipping" them by selling the improved company to another buyer or taking it public on the equity markets.

Private equity investments aren't just about buying and selling companies, however. Many private equity firms invest in debt, helping a company salvage itself by loaning it money in exchange for an equity position or another form of return. Some private equity firms target funds at startup companies—these are called venture capital firms, though a diversified private equity management company will often include venture capital activity alongside acquisitions and debt purchases. Venture capital investments are often made in exchange for equity in the private company that, the firm hopes, will turn into big profits should the startup go public or get sold.

Still, today's private equity landscape is dominated by the acquisition of once-public companies. Since 2001, 2,316 publicly traded companies have been purchased with the backing of private equity firms, a total value of $1.065 trillion, according to the National Venture Capital Association. Over the same amount of time, 384 companies were returned to the market via initial public offering (though "initial" is a bit of a misnomer since many of these companies were public once before), with the rest either sold to other companies, public or private, or remaining in the hands of private equity firms. Since 2006, the wave of private equity purchases has swallowed even bigger companies—16 companies within the Standard & Poor's 500 index have been swallowed up by private equity firms in that time period. And even among the 30 stocks comprising the Dow Jones industrial average, those blue-chip stocks said to be representative of the American economy as a whole, private equity takeover rumors swirled around such luminaries as Alcoa and Home Depot in early 2007. The record for a takeover deal's value stands at $44 billion in cash and debt, for the 2007 acquisition of utility TXU Corp. For a while, Wall Street was gearing up for the first $100 billion takeover; with the market's turmoil in the latter half of 2007, that milestone may have to wait...but it will come.

Visit the Vault Finance Career Channel at **www.vault.com/finance** - with insider firm profiles, message boards, the Vault Consulting Job Board and more.

VAULT CAREER LIBRARY

1

THE SCOOP

Private Equity Fundamentals

CHAPTER 1

Who are Private Equity Investors?

The institutions and people who invest in private equity funds are some of the wealthiest in the world. Major pension funds, such as the California Public Employees Retirement Systems (CalPERS), place some of their money with private equity funds to boost returns. Major Wall Street investment banks also place investments in private equity funds—unless, of course, they create their own in-house private equity funds as did Goldman Sachs and Morgan Stanley. Hedge funds often invest in private equity funds due to the outstanding performance these funds have amassed through the years. Indeed, a few hedge funds have blurred the line between themselves and private equity firms by taking part in public company buyouts either on their own or in partnership with more traditional private equity firms.

And finally, the firms themselves are often heavily invested in their own private equity funds. The private—and, recently, public—companies that manage private equity pools ensure their interests are aligned with those of their investors by placing a large chunk of their own wealth in the mix. This has, of course, resulted in the creation of a breed of private equity deal makers that have joined the billionaires' club, most famously Henry Kravis at KKR or current industry poster boy Steve Schwarzman of Blackstone.

The Role of the Private Equity Firm

These investors don't want to manage these big-value, big-return investments themselves. Indeed, CalPERS is outstanding at managing money and making sure millions of California retirees get their checks each month, no matter the market conditions. But do they have the expertise to find a good company to buy, run that company, and then bring it public or sell it? That's where the private equity firms—and you, potentially—come in.

A private equity firm plays multiple roles throughout a typical investment. For example:

- **Raising the fund.** The private equity firm serves as a focal point for private capital. The firm raises capital from the various constituencies mentioned above, and then manages that capital appropriately until an investment is identified. In addition, the same people who raise capital

Visit the Vault Finance Career Channel at **www.vault.com/finance**—with insider firm profiles, message boards, the Vault Finance Job Board and more.

VAULT CAREER LIBRARY 5

also help obtain credit for any leverage needed for a buyout. Finally, they manage payouts to all involved.

- **Finding a target.** Firms employ researchers whose job it is to analyze the operations of thousands of companies, looking for potential investments. Sometimes it's easy—many companies readily announce they're looking at "strategic options," business-speak for putting themselves up for sale. But there are plenty of opportunities at other companies as well, even ones that seem to be operating just fine. The researchers know the strengths of the private equity firm's various management teams, and can identify potential targets based on the firm's ability to generate even more profits from their strengths. And in still other cases, a fund may simply see a very conservative company underutilizing its resources—a chain of casual dining restaurants, for example, that hasn't leveraged the real estate it owns to the degree it could in order to expand. There are plenty of ways to find a target, which we'll discuss later on.

- **Closing the deal.** The fund must then approach the company—or, in some cases, manage a company's approach to it—and try to make a deal. This is very much like the merger-and-acquisition dance two publicly traded companies might make. The private equity firm generally hires a Wall Street investment bank for its advisory business, though its own cadre of deal-makers and due-diligence teams are often just as talented as those of the advisory firm. A deal is hammered out that usually gives the company's current shareholders a premium over the stock's current price, while giving the private equity firm enough room to make an even more impressive profit down the road.

- **Running the company.** Once a private equity firm buys a company, the deal generally fades from the news, but the hard work is just beginning. The firm, which represents the new owners, has a plan for maximizing profits ready to go—that was part of the targeting and acquisition process. The firm then brings in the individuals it thinks can execute that plan. Such plans often include a wide variety of cost-cutting measures, including new management and production processes as well as layoffs. It also typically includes borrowing quite a bit of money—generally far more than investors in a publicly traded company would stand for. As a rule, private equity firms are aggressive managers, and the leverage is put to work immediately. In recent years, that leverage has also served to give the fund's investors an early payout—essentially using the company's good name to sell bonds, the proceeds of which are then distributed to the new owners. One of the biggest debates about private equity is whether such debt is justified or even ethical, but when a company goes into private hands, there's little regulators can do.

• **The exit strategy.** There are a number of ways to unwind an equity investment and collect the profits. One is to sell the company to another entity, generally to an already-established company that was identified as a possible buyer early on in the due-diligence process. The private equity firm has done all of the hard work, after all, making it more attractive for a major corporation to buy. Alternatively, there are some companies that are simply bought for parts—there was speculation that Toys "R" Us would've been a much more profitable investment if its private equity buyers simply closed down the struggling toy retail business and sold all of its properties off. Finally and most notably, the private equity firm "flips" the company, returning it to the public equity markets through an initial public offering. In general, the company has to be stronger than it was when purchased for the private equity investors to get a good return, though in some cases—notably the Hertz IPO—the companies can be overloaded with debt. The private investors generally receive the proceeds of the IPO, though in some cases at least part of the proceeds will go to the company itself.

Naturally, when dealing with billions of dollars and major corporations, private equity firms need a wide variety of talented employees. And that's where you'll come in. Private equity firms employ some of the most experienced talent in corporate America, and their personnel needs are as broad as they are deep. Whether you're fresh out of undergrad or a seasoned corporate veteran, chances are you can find a home with private equity firms. And in doing so, you'll have a hand in making billions for your investors while guiding large corporations, and the thousands of people they employ, through major changes and improvements.

The Modern Private Equity Firm

Today, private equity firms are primarily dedicated to the purchase of companies or stakes therein. Yet some, including Bain Capital and The Blackstone Group most notably, have entered other businesses, including distressed debt and real estate. At the same time, hedge funds have started dabbling in private equity as well, mostly through placements, but occasionally through their own, active efforts as well.

Yet the average private equity firm remains dedicated to the concept of the buyout. Over the long haul, the returns from a private equity placement have yet to be rivaled consistently by any other asset class, including hedge funds.

Visit the Vault Finance Career Channel at **www.vault.com/finance**—with insider firm profiles, message boards, the Vault Finance Job Board and more.

VAULT CAREER LIBRARY   7

There simply aren't any other investments where returns can reasonably be as high. And even with questions arising about the current M&A and LBO environments, private equity funds have proven their worth to investors time and again.

Private equity in the U.S.

There are only about 200 private equity companies operating at any one time in the United States, and that number can vary due to openings and closures on the small end of the scale. But the money they manage is impressive. According to the newly created Private Equity Council—formed by firms in response to increasing pressure from Washington on their activities and profits—private equity firms were responsible for $406 billion in transactions in 2006. They had already eclipsed that mark by mid-2007.

Like their venture capital cousins, private equity firms generally find specialties within the industry. Some firms will focus on middle-market, mid-cap transactions, while others take aim at overseas purchases. Still others look at small, public companies or those within a specific sector.

And then there are the big ones. They have the money and clout to go after the biggest deals in a variety of sectors. Here's a look at the biggest and most noteworthy firms in private equity today:

The Big Names

The Blackstone Group

Arguably one of the top two firms in the world, Blackstone was started in 1985 with $400,000 and recently raised $23 billion for its buyout funds. CEO Steve Schwarzman is known as a sharp tactician. The company, which went public in 2007, recently diversified its interests beyond private equity and into hedge funds, distressed debt and real estate holdings. That's led Blackstone to have perhaps the most aggressive talent recruiting effort among private equity firms today.

Kohlberg Kravis Roberts & Co. (KKR)

One of the oldest and most successful firms, KKR is considered Blackstone's chief rival for king of the private equity hill. Founded in 1976, the firm today can boast of an average annual rate of return of 27 percent. It also has one of the most rigid corporate structures in the industry, with 11 industry groups within the company focusing on 100-day operating plans for portfolio companies and dealmaking. And the investment committee meets every Monday for a comprehensive look at the firm's operations. KKR is also perhaps the "purest" pure-play private equity firm out there, with little presence in other forms of investment.

The Carlyle Group

With $55 billion under management, Carlyle operates 48 different funds across four main investment areas: buyouts, venture capital, real estate and leverage finance. The latter has given the company trouble of late—Carlyle management had to lend its Carlyle Capital hedge fund subsidiary $200 million for a bailout brought on by the 2007 market crisis, as many of the hedge fund's investments in structured credit issues plummeted. Carlyle is one of the largest private equity firms in the world, with 750 people in 27 offices around the globe. The firm's averaged a 31 percent return rate since its founding in 1987.

Texas Pacific Group

This firm vaulted into the top echelon of private equity with its 1993 purchase of twice-bankrupt Continental Airlines—which it ultimately unloaded for more than 10 times the purchase price. It leveraged its airline expertise with an $8.7 billion purchase of Australian airline Qantas in 2006. It's building a larger presence in the Pacific Rim than most private equity firms.

Bain Capital

Bain is perhaps best known for producing Republican presidential candidate Mitt Romney, who was CEO of the company until he left in 1999 to run for governor of Massachusetts. The firm has been without a CEO since, instead relying on its 26 partners for committee-style leadership that's been surprisingly effective. The firm's been specializing in "club" deals, and recently started a $1 billion Asia fund. Many of the Boston-based firm's investors are university endowments.

Providence Equity Partners

This quiet, private equity firm cut its chops on a $63 million investment in VoiceStream Wireless in 1992, which was renamed T-Mobile and flipped to Deutsche Telekom in 2000 for 19 times the original purchase price. Its reported rate of return is now around 70 percent, though even the firm admits that's likely unsustainable. Given its notoriety, it remains a small firm— small enough for CEO Jonathan Nelson to take the entire firm to Alta, Utah, each year on a ski trip.

Apollo Advisors

The prototypical turnaround firm, Apollo can boast that 90 percent of its investments since its founding in 1990 have produced positive returns, and it's maintained a 40 percent average rate of return each year. Founder and Chairman Leon Black is said to be a master of arranging creative debt financing, thanks to his days spent as the head of M&A at Drexel Burnham Lambert in the 1980s. He'll need all his skills to navigate the new credit environment brought on by the conditions of summer 2007.

Warburg Pincus

Warburg Pincus is unusual among private equity companies in that it tends to eschew the blockbuster deal. Instead, the firm focuses on fast-growing companies with price tags under $1 billion, which it holds on to, develops and sells years later for big profits. It's also one of the oldest private equity firms on Wall Street, with roots dating back to 1939. Another major Asia player, the firm closed a $1.2 billion real estate fund in 2006—of which 60 percent is slated for purchases in Asia.

Cerberus Capital Management

Is it a hedge fund or a private equity firm? It doesn't really matter what you call it, because Cerberus is squarely among the top 10 private equity players in the world. Its strong-armed acquisitions of grocery chain Albertson's and GMAC—both of which were targeted by KKR—turned out to be just the stepping stones for its epic $7.4 billion acquisition of the Chrysler Group from Daimler AG in 2007. Yet the firm struggled to get that deal financed amid the credit crunch—and some wonder if the two-headed dog of myth bit off more than even two mouths can chew in the Chrysler deal.

Thomas H. Lee Partners

Another venerable firm, Thomas Lee started his company in 1974 with $150,000. Today, the firm—sans Lee, who left in 2005—specializes in consumer, media and business services companies, and has participated in the "club" purchases of Dunkin' Donuts and Clear Channel Communications. If you're a Harvard Business School graduate, you may have an edge here—30 out of the 38 investment professionals are alumni.

Other private equity sources

In recent years, private equity firms have seen increased competition from hedge funds and investment banks, even as both entities have given private equity firms larger and larger placements to work with.

Investment banks tend to follow trends to continue being the "one-stop shop" for institutional banking needs. Thus, the major Wall Street firms—Goldman Sachs, Lehman Brothers, Bear Stearns, Morgan Stanley, Merrill Lynch, JPMorgan Chase and Citigroup—all started private equity arms in the past decade. (To be fair, they all started or acquired hedge funds as well.) Some, like Morgan Stanley, had long been used to interesting and unusual private equity placements, while others launched private equity funds from scratch and funded them through other operations. The results have been mixed; the banks have exceptional deal makers on staff, but their expertise in turnarounds isn't as pronounced. Indeed, the jury is still out on whether these funds will last beyond the current boom.

Hedge funds have also dipped a toe into the private equity space, much as they've entered any market or asset class that promises any kind of return. A few, such as Fortress Investment Group, have done well in managing their investments. Others are simply content to put up the cash alongside an established private equity firm and allow the firm to do most of the heavy lifting.

Visit the Vault Finance Career Channel at **www.vault.com/finance**—with insider firm profiles, message boards, the Vault Finance Job Board and more.

VAULT CAREER LIBRARY

11

A Look Inside Kohlberg Kravis Roberts & Co.

Let's take a look at perhaps the most iconic private equity firm in operation today—Kohlberg Kravis Roberts & Co., whom many credit for inventing modern private equity investing. The firm was founded in 1976 by Jerome K. Kohlberg Jr. and cousins Henry Kravis and George R. Roberts. The three founders had worked together at Bear Stearns Cos. Inc. in the 1970s before quitting to form KKR.

Like many private equity firms, KKR started simple, buying up three small, relatively unknown companies in 1977, and three more the following year. KKR was different, however, in its financing, putting up less of its investors' money in transactions. Instead, KKR used—and still uses—about 25 percent of its own capital in a transaction, financing the rest through bank loans and high-yield bond issuance. Thus, its financing for a theoretical transaction might look something like this:

Cost:	$1 billion
Capital:	$250 million
Bank loan:	$250 million at 8 percent annually
Bonds:	$500 million at 10 percent annually

Let's then say that the company's turnaround takes three years, after which it is sold to a larger enterprise (or goes public) at a value of $3 billion. Here's an admittedly simplified breakdown:

Sale price:	$3 billion
Loan principal:	$250 million
Loan interest:	$60 million
Bond principal:	$500 million
Bond interest:	$150 million
Capital:	$250 million
Profit:	$1.79 billion

Of course, KKR could've simply fronted the entire $1 billion and walked away with $2 billion in profit, thus saving $210 million in interest costs. And in the 1960s and 1970s, that's what many private equity firms had been doing. What KKR was expert at doing was using its leverage to put its own capital toward multiple investments. So it could've had $2 billion in profits from a single $1 billion investment over three years—or could've made three other $250 million investments at the same time and, in three years, could theoretically have made $7.16 billion on that same $1 billion in capital.

As you can imagine, with these kind of returns, KKR quickly ramped up its transactions. It closed six different transactions in 1981, and by 1985 it had purchased the Motel 6 chain, followed a year later by the Safeway grocery stores. By 1987, Kohlberg resigned at age 61, leaving Kravis as senior partner. KKR then started looking for a new deal—and found a big one.

KKR, and Henry Kravis in particular, came to symbolize the private takeover with its $31.4 billion acquisition of RJR Nabisco in 1988. The takeover was a brutal process, with KKR facing opposition and competing bids from RJR's own management. But the lack of a guaranteed price by management and word of then-CEO F. Ross Johnson's lucrative "golden parachute" deal in the event of a buyout ultimately tipped the board's vote toward KKR's offer. The back-and-forth between KKR, the board and management were ultimately the subject of a best-selling book, *Barbarians at the Gate*, and even an HBO movie starring James Garner and Jonathan Pryce.

Surprisingly, while the deal made KKR the poster child of private equity—and, some say, corporate greed—the deal itself wasn't a great one. Many say that, amid the merger boom of the 1980s, KKR simply paid too much for Nabisco. And KKR was the victim of poor timing as well. Increasing tobacco litigation and intense competition among cigarette makers sent RJR's profits tumbling in that division. The economic downturn and recession of 1990-1991 made it more difficult for RJR to raise money in the debt markets, prompting KKR to throw in another $1.7 billion of its own money to prop up RJR's operations. Ultimately, KKR exited the investment in 1995, transferring some of RJR Nabisco's assets to another portfolio company—Borden Foods—and leaving the remnants on the open market. For its total $3.1 billion investment in RJR Nabisco, KKR was said to have barely broken even on the deal—if that. And RJR Nabisco itself was broken up and sold off to others.

Yet the ultimate failure of the investment was drawn out over at least seven years, and the sheer audacity of the deal made Kravis and Roberts the Wall Street equivalent of rock stars. Banks were perfectly happy to lend KKR increased amounts of leverage, because no matter how the investments did, the fees were worth it—investment banks and lenders walked away from the RJR Nabisco deal with $1 billion in payments, after all. And the success of KKR prompted other private equity firms, such as The Blackstone Group, Bain Capital and The Carlyle Group to get even more aggressive.

Visit the Vault Finance Career Channel at **www.vault.com/finance**—with insider firm profiles, message boards, the Vault Finance Job Board and more.

VAULT CAREER LIBRARY

13

Leveraged buyouts took a backseat to the technology boom in the 1990s, but KKR remained busy, buying up such diverse names as Spalding Holdings Corp. and Act III Cinemas Inc., and regaining its stride. Investment in its takeover funds slowed from 2000 to 2002 in the stock market's bear market, but KKR was one of the leaders in the private equity boom over the first decade of the 21st century.

That said, KKR isn't leading the barbarian hordes at the gate these days. Unlike its 1980s heyday, KKR is far more willing to team up with rival private equity firms for so-called "club deals," in which the risk and rewards of acquisitions are shared among a number of private equity funds. And the "hot-shot" role that Kravis enjoyed in the late 1980s has been taken on by The Blackstone Group's Stephen Schwarzman.

Nonetheless, KKR remains one of the leading private equity firms on Wall Street and is certainly the elder statesman of the industry. As of October 2007, the firm has completed some 318 transactions with a aggregate enterprise value of $318 billion. It currently has a portfolio of companies and investments worth $78 billion—on invested capital of $31 billion, a 2.5-times multiple.

A Brief History of Private Equity

CHAPTER 2

The Beginning

The history of private equity can be traced back to 1901, when J.P. Morgan—the man, not the institution—purchased Carnegie Steel Co. from Andrew Carnegie and Henry Phipps for $480 million. Phipps took his share and created, in essence, a private equity fund called the Bessemer Trust. Today the Bessemer Trust is more private bank than private equity firm, but Phipps and his children started a trend of buying exclusive rights to up-and-coming companies—or buying them outright.

Yet, although there were pools of private money in existence between the turn of the century and through the 1950s, these were primarily invested in startups, much like today's venture capital firms. The notion of a private buyout of an established public company remained foreign to most investors until 1958, when President Dwight D. Eisenhower signed the Small Business Act of 1958. That provided government loans to private venture capital firms, allowing them to leverage their own holdings to make bigger loans to startups—the first real leveraged purchases.

Soon, other companies started playing with the idea of leverage. Lewis B. Cullman made the first modern leveraged buyout in 1964 through the purchase of the Orkin Exterminating Co. Others followed, but the trend quickly died by the early 1970s. For one, the government raised capital gains taxes, making it more difficult for KKR and other nascent firms to attract capital. Pension funds were restricted by Congress in 1974 from making "risky" investments—and that included private equity funds.

Greed is Good: Modern Private Equity

These trends started reversing themselves in the 1980s, when Congress relaxed both pension fund restrictions and capital gains taxes. Money flowed back into private equity funds, and some of the best-known firms were founded—Bain Capital in 1984, The Blackstone Group in 1985 and The Carlyle Group in 1987.

Carl Icahn made a name for himself as a corporate raider with his LBO of TWA Airlines in 1985, and KKR raised private equity's visibility to a new high with the $31.4 billion acquisition of RJR Nabisco in 1988.

This was a time of growing pains for private equity as well as intense success. Many firms realized that they couldn't act in a bubble, as KKR found out with a ton of negative publicity surrounding the RJR Nabisco deal. Tom Wolfe's *The Bonfire of the Vanities* gave all of Wall Street a black eye, and Gordon Gecko's "Greed is good" mantra from *Wall Street* was pinned on private equity firms as a whole. By the time the 1990-1991 recession took hold, private equity firms resumed a low profile, waiting for the next boom.

The tech boom

The tech boom of the 1990s was a unique time for private equity. Stock prices soared, even for companies that had no business being publicly traded, let alone having a rising stock price. It became inordinately difficult for a private equity firm to create value through the traditional buyout method.

But at the same time, venture capital was on the rise, fueling a surge of new companies. As one venture capitalist put it at the time, "Look, I'll throw $1 million at 10 different companies. If one company succeeds, that'll bring me $50 million. So it's worth it in the end." So the major private equity firms shifted gears and participated in the boom through startup funding. LBOs still occurred, but at far less impressive levels than in the 1980s.

A maturing industry

The dot-com bust of 2000-2001 brought the markets back to reality and unearthed new opportunities for private equity firms. Some firms swept in to buy good companies on the cheap, waiting for the bust mentality to pass before returning them to market. Others simply enjoyed the fire sale, and bought technology and patents for resale, dismantling the failed companies in the process.

By 2003, the market had returned to a bull cycle, but with some notable changes. Congress had enacted the Sarbanes-Oxley Act, which tightened regulations on public companies and what they could say and do. The new bull market was very much focused on companies "hitting their numbers" instead of long-term investment in new business. Those pressures combined to make private buyouts seem attractive to potential target companies.

Furthermore, the rise of hedge funds created a great deal of wealth that needed new homes, and broadened the number of potential investors in private equity. Soon, newly wealthy individuals, hedge funds and major Wall Street institutions were all piling into private equity, and the firms enjoyed even more success, leveraging their newfound capital into major multibillion-dollar deals. The record RJR Nabisco buyout was eclipsed twice in 2007 alone.

The Summer of 2007

Early on, 2007 was shaping up to be a remarkable year for private equity firms. Private investors LBO'ed the nation's largest utility, TXU Corp., in a record $44.3 billion private buyout that had the heads of Blackstone and KKR gladhanding members of the Texas Legislature in what many saw as a symbol for private equity's increasing clout.

Then, in the summer, the whole private equity wave came crashing down. And it wasn't even the firms' fault. LBOs became the latest victim of the housing and mortgage crisis.

Where it began

Ever since the dot-com crash and subsequent recession of 2000-2002, investors disillusioned with high-flying stocks started investing in tangible assets, mostly real estate. By 2004, the condo-flipping craze was in full swing. Prices had soared considerably in just three to four years—threefold in places like Los Angeles, Las Vegas and Miami. The national banking system helped fuel the craze with mortgages supported by historically low interest rates and relatively easy terms.

But in June 2004, the Federal Reserve started raising interest rates, which went from 1 percent at the start of 2004 to 5.25 percent in July of 2006, where they remained. Yet housing prices continued to climb as speculators jumped in and out of house purchases. That left the average homeowner struggling to afford a home. In response, mortgage lenders started pushing unusual mortgage products—everything from 50-year mortgages to interest-only, adjustable-rate loans. And because home prices had been on such a strong trajectory, many banks relaxed their lending requirements for "subprime" mortgages—loans to high-risk, poor-credit borrowers. The reasoning was that even these borrowers could refinance once their home prices appreciated substantially.

Visit the Vault Finance Career Channel at **www.vault.com/finance**—with insider firm profiles, message boards, the Vault Finance Job Board and more.

VAULT CAREER LIBRARY   17

The fall

The irrational exuberance in housing started falling apart in spring and summer 2006, when prices leveled off and luxury homebuilders, responsible for half-filled communities of McMansions around the country, started lowering the profit forecasts. Housing prices evened out, then started falling in the majority of cities around the country. And all of those adjustable-rate mortgages began adjusting higher. Without the expected jump in home value, many borrowers, especially those with subprime mortgages, couldn't refinance and were stuck with payments they could no longer afford.

The effect of all of the late payments, loan defaults and home foreclosures wasn't limited to mortgage brokers and banks. Many mortgage lenders packaged their loans into mortgage-backed securities—bonds backed by the expected inflow of payments from borrowers as well as the value of the homes mortgaged. But with borrowers defaulting and home prices falling, the value of these bonds dried up. And the big banks and hedge funds holding this paper found themselves hit hard. Bear Stearns had to close two billion-dollar hedge funds in June because of the hit these bonds took, and Goldman Sachs spent $2 billion of its own money in August to prop up another fund.

And, of course, both hedge funds and major banks were hit not only with depreciating mortgage-backed securities, but also a severe correction in the equity markets and bond yields that finally normalized after nearly two years of inversion.

Squeeze down

The result of all of this was a general tightening of credit. Nearly all major investment banks had mortgage-backed investments, and those with consumer arms also felt the pinch from mortgage defaults. Hedge funds, the other major source of leverage, faced the bond and equity problems, along with increased redemptions from worried investors.

The effects were seen as early as June, as Cerberus Capital Partners had difficulty borrowing the $12 billion needed to buy the Chrysler Group. It got the financing, but at less beneficial terms than it had thought. And it's unlikely that the new ownership will find underwriters to help lever Chrysler's dwindling assets for investor payoffs, let alone the capital the struggling automaker needs to keep making cars.

The lack of credit for buyouts has hurt other deals. The Home Depot Inc., once considered a prime buyout candidate itself, ended up accepting $8.5

billion to sell off its HD Supply wholesale/contractor chain to private equity buyers—the original bid was $10.5 billion. That's less money Home Depot can use for stock buybacks and dividends, further pressuring stocks and, potentially, prompting banks and hedge funds to decrease cash output.

As of the end of August 2007, there were 51 private equity deals pending, including TXU's and other notables: a consortium's $27.3 billion deal for Alltel Corp., KKR's $27 billion offer for First Data Corp. and Blackstone's $26.7 billion bid for Hilton Hotels. There is, of course, no way these deals can get done without borrowing. And if the private equity firms can't get the money on terms to their liking, they'll walk away.

"We can't borrow at unreasonable rates, but at the same time, we don't want to see too many deals fall through," says one insider at a top-three firm, who didn't want his name to be used. "If you see a bunch of us drop these megadeals, the people who have given us money are going to be really disappointed, and they're not going to give us any more. So even fewer deals will get done. It's probably the touchiest situation we've faced as an industry."

Going Public

Fortress Investment Group Inc. (FIG) was the first major company with a private equity component to go public. Fortress is very much a hybrid of hedge fund and private equity, and is widely seen as more the former than the latter. Nonetheless, Fortress raised $643 million in its February 12, 2007 initial public offering. But the worries that plagued the financial sector have taken their toll on Fortress' stock—as of late October 2007, it was down 35 percent from its April 19, 2007, high of $33.07.

Yet Fortress didn't get nearly as much attention with its IPO as did The Blackstone Group. The hottest private equity firm on Wall Street went public on June 25, 2007, trading under the ticker BX. Sadly, the timing couldn't have been worse—the market hit its peak July 19 before falling on credit concerns. Given Blackstone's reliance on easy credit, this hurt the stock—it was down 27 percent from its first day of trading as of late October. The troubled trading environment led KKR to postpone its own public offering plans.

Visit the Vault Finance Career Channel at **www.vault.com/finance**—with insider firm profiles, message boards, the Vault Finance Job Board and more.

V∧ULT CAREER LIBRARY   **19**

Public trading means public attention

The general public learned a lot about how private equity firms operate through Blackstone's prospectus. For example, the firm's profits are derived from the increasingly standard 2-and-20 fee structure, though with some surprisingly investor-friendly twists. Blackstone charges a management fee of anywhere from 1 to 2 percent on funds as they're being invested. But after the funds are placed, that fee drops to 0.75 percent. Likewise, Blackstone will take 20 percent of any returns on the investments it makes as a performance fee—but only after the fund's other investors reach their benchmark rates of returns, usually a minimum of 7 to 9 percent. If they don't reach the benchmark, Blackstone gets nothing by way of performance. And Blackstone has to repay fees if returns fall below that threshold later down the road.

Blackstone isn't shy about the nature of its business, noting that quarterly profits can be very choppy, and depend largely on attracting new money and its funds' performance. The IPOs of both Fortress and Blackstone were well subscribed, naturally, given the private equity craze of the first half of the year. Their fall since then is likewise unsurprising.

Looking to the Future

Given the market outlook outlined above, it may be tough to be overly bullish on private equity firms right now. But even during the worst market cycles of the last three decades, private equity firms remained busy, buying companies and generally going about their business. Like most things on Wall Street, private equity experiences boom and bust cycles. The boom since 2003 has been unprecedented, and private equity investors, management and employees made billions. If the boom ends in the near future, private equity firms will likely make what acquisitions they can, and then scale back fund raising and operations for a few years until things improve again. They won't be going away ... just retrenching.

How Private Equity Works

CHAPTER 3

Private equity generally works the same way throughout Wall Street, whether we're talking about an independent private equity firm, a newly public firm like The Blackstone Group, or a fund that's part of a major investment bank or hedge fund. Private equity companies, or divisions, have to create a fund and finance it, find potential investments, line up additional financing, make the deal, fix up the company and determine the exit strategy. Here's a look at how it works.

Creating a Fund

Private equity firms can have multiple funds running at the same time. Some are specialized, say in distressed debt or venture capital, while others are simply giant pools of cash the firm can use for any investment it sees fit. To create a fund, of course, the firm has to find cash.

Show me the money

A well-established private equity firm has reasonably dependable sources of capital for its funds. Major banks, pension funds, hedge funds and other Wall Street stalwarts are generally willing to give a fund several hundred million dollars each to get it started. Major universities and charities are also good sources of funds, since their endowments generally aren't used for operational purposes. Finally, private wealth management organizations sometimes pool the money of some of their high-net-worth clients—and generally only those who can measure their worth in the hundreds of millions—in order to make a private equity investment.

And of course, the managing directors and ownership of the private equity firm also puts capital into any given fund. For successful private equity investors, that can be valued at several hundred million dollars.

All of these sources of capital, pooled together, create the private equity fund. Major private equity firms can have more than $10 billion in assets, though outside a handful of these top firms, such funds tend to be in the $2 billion to $5 billion range.

Visit the Vault Finance Career Channel at **www.vault.com/finance** - with insider firm profiles, message boards, the Vault Finance Job Board and more.

VAULT CAREER LIBRARY 21

Why invest?

The funds operate much like a mutual fund, in that each participant or entity receives a return on its investment commensurate with the performance of the fund and how much each institution put in. Yet there are notable differences. Private equity firms require major commitments of time for each investment—you can't get your money back for anywhere from three to five years, for starters. That's roughly the same lifespan of a major private equity investment, and the private equity firm won't be able to execute on its strategy without assurance that the money will be there.

Depending on the kind of fund, there may be regular payouts for its investors, but in many cases, investors may have to wait the full term before getting their returns. It's because of this wait, in part, that private equity investors start levering up their new acquisitions almost immediately upon purchase. Yes, some of the capital is used to expand the business and make the changes that will bring about greater profits—but some is used simply to give investors a chunk of their money back shortly after the investment is made.

Finding a Target

Research

Once a fund is created, the private equity firm then needs to find appropriate investments. Depending on the market environment, the time this takes can vary between weeks and years. Until a target is found, the fund's resources are generally put into relatively safe investments, such as high-grade corporate bonds, blue-chip equities or Treasuries.

Private equity firms are constantly researching possible investments, even before the funds are created. These possibilities, in part, are major selling points for potential investors, who need to be reassured that the fund can put their capital into action as efficiently as possible.

Few private equity firms have the kind of massive staff of analysts on hand to do research on the bulk of publicly traded companies around the globe. Instead, they depend on the major investment banks for basic research, then go through daily reports with a fine-toothed comb for signs of possible investment. Some potential targets are easy to spot—the companies that put themselves up for sale, will attract interest, though these are by no means certain. Some companies may simply not be worth the time and money needed to turn them around. Even among publicly traded companies, there's such a thing as a bad company.

There are also companies that privately court private equity bidders. Generally, these contacts aren't made via press release, but are done quietly, with the head of M&A for a major Wall Street firm making a call to a private equity firm's managing director. Often, the company's books are laid open to the private equity firm's researchers, who can then determine if there are enough efficiencies to be gleaned to make an acquisition worthwhile.

The diamond in the rough

In still other cases, private equity firms will explore companies through their public filings and Wall Street analysts' research, and go to them independently with the potential of a takeover. In some cases, these companies may not have given much thought to a leveraged buyout—perhaps they had a longer-term plan to achieve the efficiencies that a private equity firm could make happen much faster, or perhaps they didn't even see the potential for the kinds of major improvements a private equity firm might propose. Sometimes a company is the perfect adjunct to another of the private equity firm's portfolio companies, and the firm seeks to create a private merger between the two, which would boost the value of both once they're rolled out into the open market.

Occasionally, a private equity firm will spot opportunity in a previously announced deal between two public companies or an LBO by a competitor. If the research shows the company could do a better job of creating value than the existing bidder, the private equity firm might jump in with a higher offer.

And that's the key to the entire research process—creating value. The private equity firm's demonstrated expertise must fit well with the target company's opportunities, and there must be a relatively quick "fix" that will bring the fund's shareholders value within the three- to five-year time frame. Most firms have several dozen potential opportunities on their "wish list" at any given time, just waiting for the last few pieces of the puzzle to fit into the investment scheme. Sometimes it's a question of an anticipated failure in a division, other times it's simply waiting for the stock price to fall enough to make a deal worthwhile.

Visit the Vault Finance Career Channel at **www.vault.com/finance**—with insider firm profiles, message boards, the Vault Finance Job Board and more.

VAULT CAREER LIBRARY   23

Making the Deal

The offer

When the opportunity seems ripe, the researchers and deal makers work together to create a buyout offer. This offer doesn't simply include a per-share price, but rather is a detailed plan for the company over the life of the buyout firm's involvement. To a degree, it includes the areas in which the private equity firm can bring additional value to the company, as well as how much the firm plans to invest in the company's operations. Not all the cards are laid out on the table, however. "You don't want to just spell out exactly how they can unlock billions in value," says one longtime private equity negotiator, who asked not to be identified for fear of giving those across the table from him an advantage. "You want to tell them the value is there, and maybe lowball it some, but you want them believing that you're the only one who can dig it out."

Haggling over the terms

All of the usual tricks and ploys used in traditional M&A deal making are on display in a leveraged buyout. Both sides can use Wall Street analysts and the broader media to bolster or hurt the target's share price. The futures of top management at the target firm must be taken into account. Projections of cost savings are bandied back and forth. But in addition to the typical deal-making tactics and rhetoric, private equity firms have a few aces up their sleeve that a public company buyer might not.

For one, private equity buyouts, in many cases, preserve the target company's identity; it's not getting swallowed up by a larger rival. They also give current management an opportunity to right the ship without the scrutiny that comes from being a publicly traded company. Since the dot-com bubble burst in 2000-2002, many investors have become increasingly insistent that companies "make their numbers" each quarter, surpassing quarterly revenue and profit estimates from Wall Street analysts. If they miss estimates, the stock is punished—sometimes severely. Privately, some CEOs have complained that the drive to make their numbers has hampered their ability to make the necessary long-term investments to drive long-term growth of their businesses. Instead, they hit their numbers and store up cash on their balance sheets to use in share buyback programs and higher dividends to appease public shareholders.

The other side: private owners

To have a private owner willing to invest for even a three- to five-year time frame would seem like a vacation. And the ability to put free capital back into the company is just good business. It can be a compelling mix, even for the healthiest company.

And for companies not so healthy, a buyout can be a boon in other ways. For one, the infusion of capital from private equity owners can bring about big changes in a short amount of time. Private ownership can also handle the more unpopular chores related to a turnaround, including layoffs and dealing with past creditors. The private ownership can also help top managers save face, especially if they were responsible for distressing the company in the first place. A top manager whose policies may have failed can still leave with his or her reputation intact by creating shareholder value for a buyout, usually by getting a bid with a hefty premium over the current share price. The fact that said management also leaves with a nice golden parachute is also compelling.

How long does a deal take?

Once negotiations start, agreeing to a rough framework of a deal can take months, but in reality is a two- to four-week process—private equity firms choose their targets carefully, after all. Once an agreement in principle is reached, it's announced to the general public and the target's management gets to enjoy the subsequent boost in share price. From there, months of additional negotiations take place, during which time the private equity firm gets a complete accounting of the company's operations and financial health, and the final details on layoffs, compensation, operational adjustments and finances are all ironed out. The deal then goes to the target's shareholders for approval. Once that happens, the private equity firm pays each shareholder the agreed-upon amount per share, and the company officially becomes a private entity owned by the takeover firm.

Getting Financing

You may have already noted that the major deals announced in 2007 are far greater in value than the total value of a typical private equity fund. Welcome to the world of private equity financing, which puts the "leverage" back in leveraged buyout.

Visit the Vault Finance Career Channel at **www.vault.com/finance**—with insider firm profiles, message boards, the Vault Finance Job Board and more.

VAULT CAREER LIBRARY   **25**

It's rare that a private equity firm will simply buy a company outright with its own money. For one, even the biggest private equity fund could only manage to buy a company on the small end of the large-cap scale. And as any fund manager will tell you, it's never wise to put all your money into a single investment. So instead, the money that private equity firms raise is, essentially, seed money. To get the rest, private equity firms enlist banks and hedge funds.

Loans

There are plenty of different ways to raise leverage. The first is a simple bank loan—simple, of course, if you consider $10 billion a simple sum of money. But, in essence, the private equity firm promises to repay the bank the money borrowed with a certain amount of interest. This is generally backed by either the private equity firm's own resources or, more likely, the value of the enterprise to be purchased. In theory, if the firm defaults on the loan, the bank can go after the purchased company and/or the firm itself. In reality, this rarely happens; if there's a problem, the two sides iron out a solution that, sometimes, can even involve the bank pouring more money into the target company or private equity firm to affect a greater turnaround.

Sometimes these loans are simply that: loans from a bank. In many other cases, the private equity firm will float a corporate bond, based on the perceived value of the enterprise to be purchased. In fact, over the past few years, private equity firms have sought to lever up their new companies as much as possible. That's not simply because they want as much capital as they can get to expand the companies. At least some of that leverage goes back to the private equity fund as a "special dividend" for the people who just bought the company. Much of that new debt stays on the target company's books throughout the private takeover period and on through the exit strategy.

Here's an example, admittedly somewhat extreme, of how financing works. The Ford Motor Co. sold car rental chain Hertz Inc. to Clayton, Dubilier & Rice, The Carlyle Group and Merrill Lynch Global Private Equity for $5.6 billion in September 2005. The three private equity funds put up $2.3 billion—the rest came from debt that ended up on Hertz' balance sheet. Indeed, shortly after the sale, the private equity firms got $1 billion back in dividends. Ten months later, Hertz Global Holdings was re-introduced to the marketplace in an initial public offering that raised roughly $5 billion. The three private equity firms logged a $4 billion paper profit on the deal through more special dividends and, it should be noted, about $100 million in fees charged by the private equity firms! Hertz is still paying off the debt used by the private equity firms to buy the company in the first place.

Working with hedge funds

Over the past three to four years, private equity firms have increasingly paired up with hedge funds, essentially coming together with pools of private capital to buy out a company. The hedge fund, instead of getting a fixed amount for its investment, will often go along for the ride, hoping for the same outsized returns the private equity investors will get.

Unlocking the Company's Value

Some companies may not need to be "fixed," per se, but the whole reason they were brought private was because the private equity investors saw ways to unlock increased value within the company that wasn't being used. In the next one to five years, the private equity investors go to work on leaving the company, ideally, in a better state than they found it.

Leaving their mark

A company bought out by a private equity firm won't notice what happened the day after the deal closes, but within a year, the firm will have left an indelible mark on the company. Inefficient processes are tossed out without a second thought, activities and supply chains are streamlined, the company's workforce is often cut back (at least through attrition if not outright layoffs), and new initiatives and, in some cases, new products are introduced.

The firm's role in this stage of the process is to set definitive goals for improvement and lead the company to make those goals a reality. Targets are set—often during the deal-making process—and are reached through the leadership of the private equity firm's consultants and hand-picked managers. There are often those within the newly private company who will bemoan the changes; they're generally the ones who will be shown the exits first. Private equity firms have neither the time nor the inclination to be sentimental about their new purchases, and thus the changes that take place can be jarring and drastic. A good private equity firm, however, will take the time to get the employees to buy into the new program, which helps everyone—the employees keep their jobs and feel good about change, while the private equity firm gets a quicker and more efficient outcome.

Visit the Vault Finance Career Channel at **www.vault.com/finance**—with insider firm profiles, message boards, the Vault Finance Job Board and more.

VAULT CAREER LIBRARY   27

Pulling it off

There are, of course, an infinite number of ways to unlock value in a given company. Retail chains are popular targets of late because underperforming outlets can be closed and the real estate sold. (There was talk that Toys "R" Us would be shuttered entirely by private equity owners since the company's real estate was actually worth more than the toy business. The Times Square property alone would've been a billion-dollar parcel.) Industrial companies can be improved with new machinery and tighter supply chains. Payrolls can be reduced, debt can be restructured and a variety of expenses can be cut through using different vendors or items. New customers and contracts are pursued.

Alternatively, the "fix" may involve disbanding the company, either in part or altogether. Smaller conglomerates tend to be unwieldy—so why not focus on the core business and sell off the other divisions? Perhaps there just aren't enough synergies within the company, so the divisions can be sold off to rivals. So long as it generates capital or the potential of higher profit down the road, the private equity firm will do whatever it takes.

The Exit Strategy: Return on Investment

Private equity firms aren't in the business of actually owning companies. They buy and sell companies like one would buy an old house, fix it up and resell it for a handsome profit. At some point, the private equity firm will want to close out the investment and reap the returns. In general, it has plenty of options.

The most common way to reap the benefits is to reintroduce the company to the public market via an "initial" public offering—a somewhat misleading name since this is likely the second time the company has floated stock. Nonetheless, the company is new in the eyes of regulators, and thus is a new offering.

IPOs

The IPO route is quite similar to that of any other company seeking to go public. The private equity firm hires an investment bank (or walks across the hall, in the case of a private equity division of an investment bank) to underwrite the offering. The investment bank does an assessment of what it thinks the enterprise is now worth; ideally, the private equity firm has brought enough value to the company to make it worth more than the initial purchase price. The private equity owners and investment bank come to a consensus of value, and then the company goes on a junket with the investment bank, giving institutional investors and Wall Street analysts a "road show" to discuss how much the company has improved and what it's worth now—and, of course, what it will be worth in the years to come.

Ultimately, the company sets an offering price and a date, and stock is floated. Generally, the private equity firms will retain large chunks of equity in the company, floating anywhere from 20 to 90 percent of the stock on the open market. The proceeds of the IPO generally go to the private equity firms. Sometimes, the firms will float only a minority of the outstanding shares, leaving them with effective control of the company. The private equity firm may unwind its position in time, of course. Other times, the firm is simply interested in getting out with as much money as possible. It may hold on to a stake to see how much it appreciates, however, building even more value for its own stakeholders.

Private equity firms are partial to IPOs because they bring about returns in several stages. When the firm releases stock to the public, it receives the returns. It then gets to see its remaining stake appreciate, and can participate in dividend and stock buyback programs as well. And, as we saw from the Hertz example previously, it can find whatever additional fees it wants to end the relationship between it and the newly public company.

Other reselling tactics

The other exit strategies are fairly straightforward—outright sale and disbanding the company. In an outright sale, the "fixed up" company is sold to someone else, generally a larger public or private company. This can be somewhat less lucrative, but the company also doesn't have to be in pristine shape, either. If a private equity firm has come across some recalcitrant problems within its target company, selling to another company effectively passes off the problem while still generating returns for the firm's investors.

Alternatively, the private equity firm may opt for a sum-of-its-parts strategy, selling off the company piecemeal. This is particularly popular when a private equity firm purchases a distressed or even bankrupt company that has more than one operating unit. The units can be broken apart and sold to rivals, who are likely to pay a premium to buy up market share at the expense of a one-time rival. Some private equity firms will even purchase a company

Visit the Vault Finance Career Channel at **www.vault.com/finance**—with insider firm profiles, message boards, the Vault Finance Job Board and more.

VAULT CAREER LIBRARY   **29**

solely for the purpose of merging part of it with another portfolio company to strengthen the latter, and then sell off the rest of the former company.

This is, of course, a necessarily broad overview of how private equity deals work. As previously mentioned, there are many private equity funds that specialize in distressed debt, early-stage venture capital investing and other wrinkles. But ultimately, the roles and the process are generally the same. We'll look at some important deals later on in this book.

The Players in Private Equity

So who's doing all of this? Who makes the private equity industry run? Like the rest of the financial sector—and really, much of the American economy these days—private equity is fueled by human capital. And when an industry has as many moving parts as private equity does, it takes a breadth and depth of experience unmatched by nearly any other business today.

From finding investors and researching companies, to making the deal and executing exit strategies, a private equity firm relies on a diverse group of players. The following is a look at the various roles in a typical private equity firm.

The fund raisers and investor relations

A private equity firm won't get anywhere without money. To that end, private equity firms employ fund raisers to help attract the capital needed. These roles are quite similar to investor relations positions at public companies, institutional banks and mutual funds. Their job is to sell the ideas behind the firm's latest private equity fund, convincing major institutions—hedge funds, banks, pension funds and the like—to give the firm hundreds of millions of dollars to manage.

These people also serve as investors' point of contact. They help manage investors' accounts, let them know when they can expect returns and assuage any fears they may have. For major accounts, they also bring in some of the firm's top leadership as needed to help close major investments.

Naturally, those in these roles are exceptional salespeople with experience in dealing with major financial institutions.

The researchers

The key to unlocking value is knowing where to look, and that falls to the researchers at the private equity firm. These are the people who comb through volumes of analyst reports, news releases and articles, looking for opportunity. They investigate potential targets thoroughly for signs of possible value. They're tenacious and determined, with the ability not only to crunch numbers but also to get a "feel" for a company in admittedly subjective ways.

First, researchers identify targets. Again, some companies make it easy by putting themselves on the block or having a proxy, like an investment bank, contact the private equity firm. Other times, an article or research report on a company highlights a potential problem that the firm's experts are known for fixing, or an analyst may simply note that a company's share price has been flat for a long time. That can trigger an intensive and somewhat covert investigation into the company's fortunes. The firm's researchers gather and collate all existing Wall Street research and media reports on the company. They'll contact the company's suppliers and clients. They may even reach out to a handful of key people within the company on an informal basis.

Then, the researchers coordinate with the deal makers to agree on whether the company is a potential target. Once the company is approached and enters into negotiations, there's a whole new set of data that needs to be explored. The would-be target opens its books and operations to the firm's researchers. At that point, the firm's overall investment thesis is tested and, hopefully, proven. Some avenues of potential value are discovered, and others are abandoned.

Finally, the researchers come up with a final investment thesis for the company that serves as not only the basis for negotiations, but the agenda for the company's entire ownership. This thesis outlines areas of savings, cost-cutting plans, new ventures, the state of the company's balance sheet and how much debt it can take on—everything. The researchers come up with the plan that will ultimately be executed.

Needless to say, it takes someone with an incredible depth of knowledge to engage in this kind of work. Most have a strong financial bent, and some have spent time in corporate finance, Wall Street buy-side or sell-side research shops, or both. A few actuaries have found themselves crunching numbers for private equity firms as well.

Visit the Vault Finance Career Channel at **www.vault.com/finance**—with insider firm profiles, message boards, the Vault Finance Job Board and more.

VAULT CAREER LIBRARY   31

The deal-makers

Once a target has been identified and the investment thesis proven, the deal-makers go to work. They're the ones responsible for obtaining the company at the best possible terms. In many cases, they work not only with the target company, but also with sources of financing, including investment banks and hedge funds, to obtain the necessary leverage at low enough rates to make the deal work. They are the old-school *Masters of the Universe*, making deals worth billions that can affect the lives of thousands. This is heady stuff, to be sure.

In most firms, the chief deal-maker and the head of the firm are often one and the same. Deals don't get done, after all, until the top guy signs off on them, and men like KKR's Henry Kravis and Blackstone's Steve Schwarzman are renowned deal-makers. That's not to say that they're the ones sitting at the table—though sometimes they are if the deal's big enough. But they're directing the firm's negotiations and making sure that the deal jives with the overall investment thesis.

Some firms employ their own negotiators who answer to the company's top leadership. Other firms don't; like any other would-be buyer, many simply hire an investment bank to do the negotiating. But at most private equity firms, at least one of the firm's top managers, if not the founder, is really calling the shots at the table, while the I-bankers are there in more of a research and advisory role.

The Top Deal-Makers

At most private equity firms, the top deal-makers are synonymous with the heads of the private equity firms. Here's a look at the deal-makers who make headlines:

Henry Kravis, Kohlberg Kravis Roberts

Kravis could very well have reached "senior statesman" status among private equity investors—some say his mere presence in talks gets deals done. The firm has relied less on Kravis and fellow founding partner George Roberts these days, but is still considered neck and neck with Blackstone when it comes to which firm is leading the pack. Kravis is very focused on philanthropy, with his name on seemingly half of New York's nonprofit institutions.

Steve Schwarzman, Blackstone

Schwarzman is quickly taking up Kravis' mantle as the Gordon Gecko clone on modern Wall Street. His $400 million income makes almost as many headlines as his $5 million birthday party, and his let's-go-to-war attitude when negotiating deals. Yet thus far, the larger-than-life image works. That could change in 2008 as the newly public company's investors start complaining about the bumpy profits that Schwarzman, to his credit, warned them about.

David Bonderman, Texas Pacific Group

Bonderman is of the Schwarzman mold ... or, rather, he would say Schwarzman is from his mold. He's an old-school, leveraged buyout guy whose assistants handle his e-mail for him—he even dictates the responses—and he's also had a few headlines for his lavish lifestyle. But the hard-charging demeanor belies careful preparation and canny negotiating skills.

Steve Pagliuca, Bain Capital

Ever since Mitt Romney left Bain in 1999 to launch his political career, Pagliuca has been one of Bain's top deal-makers, leading the firm's takeover of HCA. He's quieter than most deal-makers, and prefers the intellectual approach to his colleagues' occasional bluster. And while there aren't any reports of major birthday sprees, he is part owner of the Boston Celtics.

Visit the Vault Finance Career Channel at **www.vault.com/finance**—with insider firm profiles, message boards, the Vault Finance Job Board and more.

VAULT CAREER LIBRARY

33

> ### Leon Black, Apollo Advisors
>
> Black, the firm's founder and chairman, is considered a master of debt financing and willing to take on multiple projects at once. He's among the most experienced deal-makers outside of Kravis and Schwarzman, having been in investment banking in the 1980s with Drexel Burnham Lambert.

The operators

Once a deal is done and the target becomes a portfolio company, the firm's operators go to work. Few are actually full-time employees of the private equity firm, though each portfolio company is supervised by one or more managing directors and their accompanying staffs. The private equity firm's staff acts as both top-level managers and consultants, making sure the portfolio company meets its targets, as outlined by the investment thesis, and offering advice on how to get there.

There's also a whole other level of operators that firms use: Established corporate executives who go from company to company on behalf of the private equity firm. They take on top leadership roles at the newly acquired company and get things done. These "hired guns" are generally successful C-level executives noted for their turnaround expertise and willingness to do whatever it takes to get the company where the private equity firm wants it to be.

To put it in another perspective, the private equity firm's representatives are the portfolio company's board of directors, and the hired guns take over the top-level positions and get the job done.

The in-house operators and hired guns must work together, though there have been times when the CEO installed by the private equity firm sees things differently than the researchers who came up with the investment thesis or the firm's assigned in-house operator. This is particularly true if the hired gun has more experience than the firm's assigned supervisor. This can generally be ironed out, though only after a managing director or a member of the firm's executive committee gets involved.

Hitting a moving target

All of the roles and people within a private equity firm continue to interact throughout the investment's lifespan. The researchers are often revisiting their thesis with input from operators on the ground, and the deal-makers are often pulled in to iron out the investment's exit strategy, especially if it involves a direct sale. Investor relations personnel answer questions, provide updates on investments, assuage disgruntled stakeholders and make sure everyone gets their money in the end—and can often assist in IPO road shows, too.

And of course, these are positions in firms that, generally, have fewer than 500 full-time employees around the globe. Each person at your typical private equity firm can fit into one of these roles, but they're handling multiple funds, targets, deals and/or portfolio companies. And the top managers are often shuttling between different roles—approving the investment thesis, sealing the deal, ensuring operations go smoothly and glad-handing the firm's fund investors.

Famous Big Deals

No two private equity deals are the same, because, of course, no two target companies are the same. Each transaction has its own peculiarities. Here's a look at a few notable deals that can get you started thinking about the intricacies of private equity work. Bear in mind that this list is not in any way exhaustive. Intensive reading or graduate-level course work should be on your agenda if you're interested in joining the ranks of private equity workers; there's a lot to learn from the past.

Burger King: The turnaround

At the start of the 21st century, Burger King was struggling. Its menus felt old and stale, and despite a perception of better quality food than its rivals, sales were slipping and the division as a whole lost $37 million in 2001. Its parent, Diageo, was in the beverage business—Burger King was a poor fit in the parent company's structure.

In 2002, Texas Pacific Group partnered with Bain Capital and Goldman Sachs to buy Burger King from Diageo for $1.5 billion. They were attracted by the company's brand awareness and potential for international growth, and felt that a management team asking tough questions would get results. By 2003, 15 of the division's 20 top managers were out, including Burger King's CEO. Their replacements tackled problems such as menu pricing and long drive-thru wait times. Same-stores sales jumped 33 percent by 2007 and the number of franchises in financial distress fell from 2,540 in 2003 to 60 in 2005—though part of that came from closing underperforming stores. The

Visit the Vault Finance Career Channel at **www.vault.com/finance**—with insider firm profiles, message boards, the Vault Finance Job Board and more.

V/\ULT CAREER LIBRARY   **35**

company's marketing was revamped with its core 18- to 34-year-old male "superfan" in mind.

To be fair, the new ownership piled on debt; Burger King had $1.35 billion in outstanding debt in 2006. That's since been reduced to $872 million as of March 31, 2007 and continues to dwindle. Some of the debt the company took on went into revamping it—and some went to the private equity funds.

By 2006, Burger King re-entered the market via an IPO and was valued at $2.2 billion—$700 million better than what the private equity firms paid for it. Today its market cap is $3.5 billion. Nearly three-fourths of the company is still owned by institutional holders, including the three private equity firms. Burger King is an example of a fairly typical private equity turnaround— about four years from purchase to IPO, added debt, better operations and solid prospects for long-term growth.

AutoZone: A long-term deal

The story of auto parts retailer AutoZone is unusual in that KKR held on to the company for 12 years. Sometimes, it takes a while for a company to come into its own, and KKR's stake was small enough that it could wait for its return.

AutoZone was a five-year-old subsidiary of a wholesale grocer in 1984 when its owner, J.R. Hyde, approached KKR about helping to fund a management-led buyout. KKR agreed, putting up $115 million along with the $35 million Hyde and other managers were paying, and the firm helped arrange roughly $550 million in leverage to complete the buyout of both the auto parts arm and the wholesale grocer.

In two years, the then "Auto Shack" stores expanded from 160 to 335. The company instituted a direct-order service, a lifetime guarantee on virtually all parts, and an electronic catalog and inventory system. By 1987, the wholesale grocer business was sold off so KKR and the management team could focus on the rapidly expanding parts business.

In 1991, AutoZone IPO'ed as a new company, though KKR kept a major stake, and a strong hand in operations, for the next five years. When it exited the investment in 1996, the company had grown from 1,000 employees and 160 stores to 27,000 employees and 1,400 stores. Today it owns more than 3,700 stores and has a market cap of $7.51 billion. For its part, media reports peg KKR's return on its investment at more than $2 billion.

TWA: Good for the buyer, bad for the company

In 1985, legendary corporate raider Carl Icahn, basically a one-man private equity firm, successfully LBO'ed Trans World Airlines. And like a private equity firm, he immediately set about streamlining the company and wringing out value where he could find it. The difference between Icahn's takeover and that of a typical private equity buyout is that Icahn was perhaps even more focused on the bottom line—his—than a private equity firm might be.

Icahn immediately alienated the airline's unions. The local chapter of the International Federation of Flight Attendants went on strike in 1986 rather than accept a contract from Icahn that called for a 22 percent wage cut—a stunning move given Icahn's union backing in the takeover. Icahn also sold off lucrative international air routes to rival airlines and pared back purchases of new aircraft. Finally, TWA went into Chapter 11 bankruptcy, emerging in 1993 with Icahn leaving (with an estimated $500 million in profits) the company ownership in employee hands. As part of the post-bankruptcy transfer of ownership, Icahn loaned TWA $150 million in operating costs and got a massive opportunity—the company agreed to sell Icahn an unlimited number of airline tickets at a steep discount—45 percent in many cases. Soon, a web outfit Icahn had set up was filling up to 78 percent of TWA flights with steeply discounted tickets. It's no wonder that TWA went bankrupt again in the late 1990s and sold itself to American Airlines in 2001.

TWA is worth mentioning only as a cautionary tale. Icahn rightly believed in the primacy of increasing shareholder value, but essentially gutted the company to do it. In the eight years he was in charge, he made millions but put his company into bankruptcy, then had a deal that weighed on the company's chances for years to come. Private equity firms like the idea of increasing value, but prefer to leave the company standing on its own two feet—or sold off entirely to someone else—when it's done.

U.S. Office Products—Bad all around

Sometimes, the strategies just don't work. Clayton, Dubilier and Rice Inc. purchased a controlling stake in a company called U.S. Office Products Co. in 1998 for $270 million—the rest of the company remained public. The company's founder and board member, Allon H. Lefever, was said to be on board with the buyout, according to *BusinessWeek*, because of the expertise and money Clayton had. Indeed, U.S. Office Products was a mini-conglomerate of its own, with some 100 companies under the publicly traded U.S. Office Products umbrella. Clayton felt there was plenty of opportunity

Visit the Vault Finance Career Channel at **www.vault.com/finance**—with insider firm profiles, message boards, the Vault Finance Job Board and more.

VAULT CAREER LIBRARY   **37**

for cost cutting and streamlining. The company seemed to be in good fiscal shape. Perhaps some businesses would be sold off to rivals, others would form the core of a revamped company—or companies—and then a stock offering or two later, and Clayton would be out with a tidy profit. It was to be the quick flip—shuffle through the holdings, find what works, fire-sale the rest and exit within three to five years.

It started off well. Clayton brought in a new chairman, "Jack Welch disciple" Charles P. Pieper. Tyco International CEO Dennis Kozlowski—known at the time for his merger and acquisition acumen, rather than his tasteless parties and expensive housewares—joined the board. The company stopped its acquisition tear and started cutting costs.

Pieper, however, was the prototypical private equity operator, sitting on multiple Clayton-owned company boards. When U.S. Office Products' CEO went to a dot-com startup in 1999, Pieper took on that role as well. Many people close to the deal told reporters that Pieper was spread too thin to lead such a diverse company.

The problem Pieper and others discovered was that acquisitions had inflated the company's earnings, so the remnant of the company that was still publicly traded was hammered on Wall Street. Top employees started leaving for better jobs. Clayton had to rush in with another $51 million in 1999 to stop the losses from harming the company's debt. It didn't matter: By March 2001, U.S. Office Products filed for bankruptcy, and Clayton had lost $320 million.

In retrospect, Clayton didn't see how U.S. Office's acquisition spree had juiced its earnings. Cost-cutting wasn't the answer—stopping the acquisitions exposed the flaw. Debt piled up, and the component companies just weren't producing enough cash flow to cover it. Combined with a stretched-thin leadership and the distraction of the imploding dot-com bubble, the exit strategy went from cutting and flipping to Chapter 11.

GETTING HIRED

What Are Private Equity Firms Looking For?

CHAPTER 4

Until the renaissance in hedge funds over the last decade, private equity firms were truly the *Masters of the Universe* of Tom Wolfe fame. Since then, however, private equity has had to compete with high-paying hedge funds for talent. Thankfully, the two industries are in, for the most part, different businesses, so the competition has been more for up-and-coming talent than the experienced people private equity firms tend to prefer.

And experience is key here. An MBA graduate with decent marks from a good school can reasonably expect to find an associate's position waiting for him or her at a big Wall Street firm of some kind. Yet at most private equity shops, that person would be told to come back with 20 years of increasingly important and productive experience.

"Given a choice between hiring an experienced investor for our firm and landing a guy who's run a leveraged buyout, I'd take the latter," The Carlyle Group's co-founder, David Rubenstein, told *Fortune* in 2007.

That's not to say you can't land a position at a private equity firm as a newly minted MBA, or even fresh from undergraduate school. But it's rare, and only a handful of private equity firms have a few openings for candidates at this level of experience. But don't despair. The sheer diversity of operations within a typical private equity firm provides a number of opportunities for you. And if you don't get in the door right out of college, you can position yourself for a private equity career while working elsewhere.

Here's a look, broadly speaking, at what private equity firms seek in new hires:

Education

To MBA or not to MBA?

Again, with only a handful of exceptions, such as The Blackstone Group's analyst program for undergraduates, an MBA is about as close to a prerequisite for most private equity positions as you can get. And unless you're coming on board with top-notch experience at a big-name Wall Street firm, that MBA needs to be from a high-ranked school. Higher degrees, however, are seen as a luxury, so you won't find too many doctorates among private equity employees. But in addition to the MBA, you'll be expected to

Visit the Vault **Finance** Career Channel at **www.vault.com/finance**—with insider firm profiles, message boards, the Vault Finance Job Board and more.

VAULT CAREER LIBRARY   41

keep up with the latest news in the field as well as some of the academic work being produced that has an impact on private equity activity.

It should be worth noting that, for many young professionals involved in trading, obtaining an MBA has been seen as a waste of time. A recent headline in *The New York Times* trumpeted "Bye, Bye B-School." And for those in hedge funds and other heavy-trading environments, this can certainly be true. Math and engineering backgrounds have become far more valued than traditional MBAs by some hedge funds and investment banks.

Yet among the deal-makers, there's a lot more to identifying, acquiring, streamlining and exiting a strong investment. The MBA remains an important part of the makeup of a private equity employee. Yes, in some instances, your undergraduate work and some extensive deal making and/or operational experience will help you get a job with a private equity firm. Certainly, some of the smaller and more aggressive firms are willing to overlook a master's-level degree.

Most aren't, however. So if you want to work in private equity and have yet to gain your MBA, you will have to make a very compelling case based on your experience … or start taking classes.

Experience

When you're managing funds worth $5 billion and can "lever up" as much as six times that amount, you can afford the best. And no matter what the role, private equity firms want experienced minds, even at levels that other Wall Street firms might call "entry level." For typical associate-level positions, you'll need an MBA and anywhere from two to five years of experience at a top-notch employer working directly in your specialty, whether it's deal-making, research, corporate operations, accounting, etc.

Personality Type

Private equity firms may have lost a touch of their cachet on Wall Street to hedge funds, but they've lost none of their swagger. "We are in the business of flipping entire companies," one private equity deal-maker said with candor. "You have to have the brains to see the opportunity, the balls to take it and the guts to make the investment work, even if it means cutting jobs or somehow being the bad guy everyone at the (target) company hates."

Confidence, the prototypical "can-do" attitude and an awareness of the exigencies of the job at hand are all critical to success in private equity.

For one, there are no wallflowers at this party. You may have to ferret out details about a target company, negotiate a takeover bid or stand up to the entrenched interests at the company you're trying to streamline. And, of course, your supervisors and, ultimately, your investors will not take kindly to the word "no," so you'll need to be both stubborn and creative when dealing with problems. Finally, successful private equity players are almost hyperaware of what they're doing and what's swirling around them. You may be in charge of streamlining labor costs at a portfolio company, but you need to be able to see the fact that the production lines could benefit from new technology, for example. Private equity firms create value, and you need to be on the lookout for ways to do that in any way possible.

Your private equity career path

We've discussed the various roles and opportunities in private equity firms in Chapter 3, so you probably have a sense of what you'd like to do in the field. Most of the roles in private equity have counterparts in the larger financial sector, so the best way to aim for a private equity position is to gather the kind of experience the firms are looking for in the role you seek.

Most new hires in private equity firms come from the investment banking divisions of major Wall Street firms like Morgan Stanley or Lehman Brothers. There, you'll gain valuable experience and perspective on deal-making at a variety of levels and can see how both buyers and sellers in M&A manage their bids. You may even become involved in an M&A deal involving a private equity firm's bid for the bank's client, which not only provides valuable experience related to your future industry, but could also give you a few good contacts as well!

The majority of researchers and deal-makers come from investment banks, but those responsible for managing portfolio companies can run the gamut. Anyone who's worked at a major company in areas of cost-cutting, business analysis or operations is a good candidate for private equity firms as well. These people are sometimes drawn from the ranks of portfolio companies, but firms will also hire a proven cost-cutter or streamliner to oversee operations for a number of companies.

Visit the Vault Finance Career Channel at **www.vault.com/finance**—with insider firm profiles, message boards, the Vault Finance Job Board and more.

V∧ULT CAREER LIBRARY   **43**

Finding the Job

Many people working in private equity today joke that the job found them, not the other way around. The firms were small, nimble and only needed a few key people to operate, as so many of their other functions were outsourced to consultants and specialty shops. "I was on the team at an investment bank that had represented a target company in an LBO," says a deal-maker now working for one of the top-five private equity firms in the world. "I wasn't even the lead guy, but I had come up with something that caused my client's company to be valued substantially higher than anyone had thought. After the deal closes, my phone rings. It's the head of the (private equity) firm, and he's talking about salary and bonus money that I'd never thought I'd see in my career."

Breaking into Wall Street

Despite astronomical growth throughout the finance sector in the past 20 years, the Wall Street deal-making community remains very much a tight-knit fraternity. (And fraternity is indeed the right word; there's little dependable data to go on, but for all practical purposes, women in private equity are rare. However, the majority of firms have actively tried to recruit women.) Openings in private equity firms aren't an everyday occurrence, except at the largest, which used the private equity boom of the 2000s to expand aggressively around the world. Indeed, for younger and more inexperienced candidates, the larger firms may provide the best opportunities to latch on at a private equity firm.

For years, private equity firms gave little thought to actually posting job openings, let alone recruiting talent right out of college, or even out of MBA programs. They had plenty of capital to use in hiring the absolute best and brightest on Wall Street. "There was a time, particularly in the mid-to-late 1980s, when private equity was the pinnacle of deal making on Wall Street— that whole *Barbarians at the Gate*, *Masters of the Universe* thing," said one longtime managing director of a private equity firm.

Yet today the pool of available talent has been spread thin. Hedge funds, in particular, have attracted more and more of the experienced professionals private equity firms crave with the lure of becoming a billionaire in a short time, and even the traditional Wall Street firms and other corporations are willing to lavish millions on their best people to get them to stay put.

Visit the Vault Finance Career Channel at **www.vault.com/finance**—with insider firm profiles, message boards, the Vault Finance Job Board and more.

VAULT CAREER LIBRARY   45

Despite this, many private equity firms still keep to old hiring practices—only a small number have a "careers" section on their web sites, and a handful of top firms don't even have web sites. But over the past five years, as competition for talent has intensified, a few firms have begun a more direct, focused search for talent. "Today, we're still up there in terms of prestige, but we're up against a lot of lucrative opportunities," the managing director said. "So we have to go out and get 'em young, and grow 'em ourselves."

Women and minorities

Most private equity firms admit they would love to include more women and minorities in the mix of candidates. Some have taken strides in one or both areas, but like much of Wall Street, private equity firms remain dominated by older white men. Many firms see this as something that will merely take time to change. Turnover at many firms is low, and few are growing their employee base aggressively. As women and minorities become more experienced in deal-making and other areas of finance, they will ultimately come to the attention of private equity firms. At least, that's the thinking. For lower-level positions, women and minorities do tend to attract more interest, but only as long as they come from the firm's preferred academic environments and have strong experience.

A recent article in *Portfolio* said the private equity industry had some of the thickest glass ceilings for women in all of corporate America. The article featured a photo of six women who could be considered senior deal-makers. And of the top-10 private equity firms in the United States, there are exactly four partner-level women "charged with putting together deals," the magazine said. Women in the industry are generally reticent to talk about the inequities, but most agree they have to work harder than their male counterparts to make it to the top echelons of private equity—and you can forget any semblance of work/life balance.

Getting in the Door

The majority of this focus is on midlevel employees—analysts looking to become associates, or associates seeking to take on a greater role elsewhere instead of waiting for a VP slot to open up. And private equity firms are generally looking for more than just standard Wall Street experience. For example, take a look at this recent job posting from Bain Capital:

Associate Position Description

The associate position will be geographically located in Shanghai, Hong Kong or Tokyo. Private equity associates are involved in all elements of the private equity business. Significant activities include evaluating investment opportunities, raising debt financing, managing outside diligence specialists and working with portfolio companies to drive value creation. Highly successful associates have demonstrated the ability to execute fundamental strategic analysis, apply sound business judgment, interact as peers with senior executives and manage complex, fast-moving processes. These individuals are typically self-starters, feel a strong sense of ownership of their work, and have excellent team and interpersonal skills.

In addition, associates will benefit from a comprehensive, multi-week training program in Boston that is designed to introduce Bain Capital's value-added investment approach. Associates will learn how to evaluate investment opportunities through the application of fundamental strategic analysis in addition to the more traditional financial modeling. Bain Capital professionals are exposed to a broad set of situations and companies, and systematically develop skills as a value-added investor.

Position Qualifications

- Exceptional business analytic and quantitative skills
- One to three years of experience in consulting or investment management (minimum of four+ years total full-time work experience)
- Strong intellect and focus
- Excellent professional and academic track record
- Excellent communication skills; able to synthesize complicated analyses concisely and to articulate insightful conclusions compellingly
- Ability to operate with limited supervision
- Excellent communication skills
- Strong interpersonal skills
- Dedicated team player with a strong sense of ownership; eager to learn and work with others

LANGUAGE REQUIREMENT

Fluent Mandarin or Japanese speaker important (current focus on Mandarin Chinese and Japanese; Korean fluency accepted as well). Strong English skills.

REQUIRED EDUCATION

MBA from a highly regarded institution.

Visit the Vault Finance Career Channel at www.vault.com/finance—with insider firm profiles, message boards, the Vault Finance Job Board and more.

VAULT CAREER LIBRARY

47

It should be noted that the only associate positions advertised on Bain's site that day were for candidates with language ability for its international operations. And bear in mind that, at most Wall Street firms, an MBA graduate from a good program or an undergrad degree holder with four years of Wall Street experience can reasonably expect to be hired as an associate.

At Bain—and many other private equity firms—they'll want four years experience *on top of* the MBA.

Undergraduates

And yet a handful of private equity firms, most notably The Blackstone Group, have started to recruit on college and university campuses alongside other Wall Street firms, and under the same terms. They offer summer internships to graduates and undergraduates, as well as entry-level programs for BA/BS and MBA holders. Many on Wall Street see Blackstone's programs as a template for the rest of the private equity industry to follow. And if the money continues to pour into private equity funds in the coming years, even the most recalcitrant firms may find themselves in need of talent. So let's take a look at what Blackstone's program is like.

Internships

Between their junior and senior years of undergraduate work, business majors can apply to join The Blackstone Group for a summer internship. This 10-week program, which starts in June, gives interns exposure to each of Blackstone's businesses—corporate private equity, of course, but also the company's real estate, hedge fund and corporate financial advisory arms. Like the majority of Wall Street undergraduate internships, the process starts with campus visits in the fall of students' junior year; if Blackstone doesn't stop by your school, contact the firm directly through its web site. Applications have to be in by December, followed by a round of interviews, either at your school or via phone, followed by a spring-break interview in New York.

Analyst programs

Blackstone also offers an analyst program for undergraduates. Get going early, though—applications are due in August. Those are then followed up with presentations and interviews throughout the fall and winter and, again, a possible spring-break trip to New York for a final interview.

The analyst program consists of an initial three-week introduction to Blackstone, including both the history and operations of the firm, as well as an introduction to the firm's technology and resources. From there, you'll be assigned to your division and group, and like most Wall Street analyst positions, you'll be doing a fair amount of grunt work—writing assignments, research, database work, creating presentations, etc.

Blackstone won't say how many people are welcomed into its program. Bear in mind, however, that Blackstone employs just 400 people—60 of whom are managing directors. Unlike the major "classes" of analysts brought aboard Goldman Sachs or Merrill Lynch each year, this is a small and intensely competitive program.

Other opportunities for undergraduates

Other firms can, and do, take on exemplary undergraduate degree holders for the equivalent of analyst positions, but this is somewhat more rare. The kind of grunt work often done by analysts is simply outsourced to investment advisory firms, researchers and auditors—analysts at Morgan Stanley or PricewaterhouseCoopers end up doing that sort of work for private equity firms on a contract basis. Firms can and do hire experienced undergraduates—those with two to three years of experience in a well-established analyst program at a major institution. They're often charged with herding the contract work done by outside firms, and assisting associates and VPs with their duties.

Again, these are rarely posted jobs; word-of-mouth through business school alumni associations or plain old social networking will help you find these positions. Scour your school's alumni directory carefully for anyone who works on Wall Street in an associate position or better; chances are they can point you to someone, somewhere. If you're fortunate, you'll find someone who actually works for a firm, and your odds will increase dramatically. You also may simply have to ask around; your family's financial advisor or bank is a good place to start, as are your friends' parents. Finally, you may need to simply pick up the phone and start cold-calling firms. There's some contact information in the appendices of this book, but the *Vault Guide to Private Equity Employers* is a more exhaustive source of contacts for the serious cold-caller.

There are other alternatives to getting into a private equity firm besides simply applying to the firm. If you've been a strong undergraduate finance student, you've already likely been in contact with investment banks. Working with the investment banking arm of a Morgan Stanley—or even Baird & Co.—can be just as much of a boon for you down the road. You'll learn deal-making from some of the best in the business and likely have a

Visit the Vault **Finance** Career Channel at **www.vault.com/finance**—with insider firm profiles, message boards, the Vault Finance Job Board and more.

VAULT CAREER LIBRARY   **49**

greater role in researching prospective deals. After completing an analyst program at an investment bank and getting an MBA, you'll be in a prime position to gain entry as an associate in a private equity firm.

Likewise, working at a hedge fund could be an interesting entrée into the private equity space. Many hedge funds have private equity investing arms—note Fortress, which went public in early 2007. Hedge funds vary widely in their hiring practices, and you could very well latch on to a fund that will give you plenty of meaningful work to do in this area. The trick, of course, is choosing the right fund. See *The Vault Career Guide to Hedge Funds* for more.

Graduate students

While undergraduate recruitment is still rare, there's been a concerted effort on the parts of both private equity firms and MBA programs to promote the skills needed for success in private equity while still in graduate school. According to a recent article in *The Wall Street Journal*, some 11 percent of the 2006 MBA class at Harvard Business School went on to private equity firms. That's up from just 7 percent in the Class of 2004. Other top-notch business schools report a similar increase—but generally such increases are reserved for the top 15 or 20 schools. After that, the limited number of positions and the firms' ability to be picky narrows one's chances considerably.

Hiring programs

Again, Blackstone has taken the lead in instituting a formal associate hiring program similar to those found at larger Wall Street firms. The firm has few new positions each year, and thus targets only the top MBA programs around the country. The process starts in August and September with informational events at these target schools, followed by more formal, one-on-one interviews with the recruiter. If Blackstone doesn't show up at your school, you can submit an application at their web site, www.blackstone.com/careers/recruiting/associates.html. The firm will get back to you if it wants to follow up. And if you're not in a top MBA program, you ought to be in the top echelon of your class and focusing like a laser on the kind of skills private equity programs want.

After that, Blackstone will likely do a follow-up phone interview over the winter and, if you're a top candidate, you'll be flown to New York in the spring. Should you get the position, you'll start in early August. Again, these are a handful of positions, and at the associate level, you'll be working very closely with VPs and managing directors on some pretty intense work. You may even work directly with fund shareholders, target or portfolio companies and financiers at this level, according to Blackstone.

Internships

Blackstone also offers a summer internship for MBA students between their first and second years of school. It operates quite similarly to the analyst summer program outlined above. You won't get as much contact with clients or anyone outside the office in such a program, but you'll work very closely with top people at the firm, and if you do well, you'll be primed for a position there, or at another private equity firm, after your final year.

Other opportunities for MBAs

Other than Blackstone, however, there are more and more firms interested in hiring top MBA graduates. The majority of these firms don't have full-fledged programs in place; they hire associates on an as-needed basis and look for specific strengths based on current needs. But they're approaching top-tier business schools to help with those needs. Harvard Business School remains the top choice of many private equity firms for recruitment. It's not just the quality of the education (it is Harvard, after all), but also the fact that private equity firms have been hiring Harvard grads for generations, and the network is in place to ensure a steady stream of graduate students to many firms.

Yet other schools are actively trying to horn in on Harvard's near-monopoly. Dartmouth's Tuck School of Business is heavily promoting its MBA program in conjunction with its Center for Private Equity and Entrepreneurship. The University of Chicago's Graduate School of Business and the University of Pennsylvania's Wharton School are also actively recruiting would-be private equity MBA candidates. Columbia University offers a "master class" in private equity, open to just 36 grad students; the school is also working to pair executive MBA candidates already working in private equity with full-time MBA students in order to further network.

Visit the Vault **Finance** Career Channel at **www.vault.com/finance** - with insider
firm profiles, message boards, the Vault Finance Job Board and more.

V∧ULT CAREER LIBRARY **51**

Sample Resumes

Undergrad for entry-level/analyst position

This is a fairly typical resume from a just-graduated undergrad seeking an entry-level position in private equity.

OBJECTIVE	To obtain an analyst position at a private equity firm or the private equity division of a financial firm or hedge fund in New York
EDUCATION	Bachelor of Business Administration in Finance, May 2008 Wharton School of Business, University of Pennsylvania Philadelphia, PA Graduated cum laude with a 3.4 GPA
EXPERIENCE	Summer analyst program, May 2007 to August 2007 Morgan Stanley, New York, NY

- Participated in the highly selective summer analyst program within Morgan Stanley's investment banking division
- Aided associates in preparing briefing books for Morgan Stanley's private equity client in the acquisition of a Fortune 1000 corporation
- Developed several research processes that helped the investment bank better perform cash-flow analyses

Summer researcher, May 2006 to August 2006
Century 21 Citywide Realty, Des Moines, IA

- Provided research assistance for the largest real estate broker in the state
- Created databases of past and present customers for use in future marketing

INTERESTS	• Wharton Undergraduate Investment Club • Sigma Alpha Epsilon fraternity • Low-income savings not-for-profit program in Philadelphia

MBA graduate for associate position

This is a good example of a better-than-average MBA graduate seeking an associate-level position.

OBJECTIVE	A challenging and rewarding position as an associate or the equivalent at a private equity firm or a division dealing with private equity buyouts or operations
EDUCATION	Masters of Business Administration, May 2008 Harvard Business School, Harvard University, Cambridge, MA Graduated magna cum laude with a 3.6 GPA Bachelor of Arts in Economics, May 2006 New York University, New York, NY Graduated summa cum laude with a 3.85 GPA
EXPERIENCE	Summer associate program, May 2007 to August 2007 BlackRock Inc., New York, NY • One of 10 MBA candidates selected for summer program at the nation's premier private equity firm • Performed operational labor analysis for three portfolio companies, identifying a total of $84 million in annual savings through eliminating redundancies and streamlining work flow procedures • Aided in analysis of labor operations at two potential buyout targets Habitat for Humanity, May 2006 to August 2006 Katrina operations center, New Orleans, LA • Aided in grant writing, accounting and operations for Habitat's largest-ever construction effort • Ensured materials and labor were on-site for each of 50 different home sites, coordinating an average of five construction projects per week • Provided final accounting for each project and, on average, brought materials costs down 15 percent through active charitable recruiting and obtaining new grants Summer analyst program, May 2005 to August 2005 Bear Stearns Cos. Inc., New York, NY • One of 20 undergraduates selected for summer undergraduate program at one of Wall Street's top investment banks • Assigned to investment banking arm and aided in analysis of client's takeover offer from private equity firm by creating potential operational scenarios • Researched other potential buyout opportunity for one of Bear Stearns' private equity clients

Note that this candidate opted to include a summer of work in New Orleans with the Katrina rebuilding effort as job experience, rather than charitable work. The work is indeed laudable, but the candidate also managed to hone her operational skills through this challenging position.

Visit the Vault Finance Career Channel at **www.vault.com/finance** - with insider firm profiles, message boards, the Vault Finance Job Board and more.

VAULT CAREER LIBRARY   53

Experienced associate with MBA for experienced-associate position

Finally, this resume is from an experienced associate with a hedge fund who's opted to try his hand at private equity.

OBJECTIVE	To obtain an experienced associate-level position with a top private equity firm
EDUCATION	Masters of Business Administration, May 2005
	Anderson School of Business, University of California at Los Angeles, Graduated cum laude with a 3.37 GPA
	Bachelor of Arts in Psychology, May 2003 University of California at Davis, Graduated magna cum laude with a 3.6 GPA
EXPERIENCE	Senior associate, D.E. Shaw & Co, New York, NY June 2005 to present

- Deputy head of major investment research, responsible for identifying companies in which the fund may take and build strong minority stakes
- Led the research effort for the fund in its partnership with two private equity firms to take Distressed Inc. private in a club deal
- Led a team of four analysts and a junior associate

Summer associate program, Merrill Lynch & Co.,
New York, NY   May 2004 to August 2004

- Spearheaded new distressed debt valuation models for the firm's private equity arm
- Aided in researching three investment banking deals on behalf of corporate and private equity clients

Summer analyst program, Baird & Co,
New York, NY   May 2002 to August 2002

- Conducted valuation research for middle-market M&A advisor and investment bank
- Assisted in preparing negotiation terms and briefing materials in deals to be closed

The Long Way Around

The vast majority of those working in private equity today didn't start there. Those who founded the firms almost invariably came from an investment banking background, while the people helping close deals today are from the legal, accounting, asset management, research and, yes, investment banking worlds. There are also those who proved themselves as "change agents" in various corporate settings and have been taken in by private equity firms as operations gurus.

So if you're an undergrad or MBA candidate who hasn't had luck getting in to a private equity firm yet, you're going to be OK. Most private equity firms would simply recommend that you latch on to a strong, reputable firm in a department or area that suits not only the private equity firms' needs, but your own talents as well. The diverse holdings and divisions within Bear Stearns or Lehman Brothers are well suited to the kinds of skills you'll need. If you're hoping to eventually end up at a private equity firm, you could do far worse.

Know where you want to be

You should bear in mind the various roles within private equity firms when you choose a program and plan your career. If you want to be a deal-maker and/or a financier, then investment banking is the obvious choice. If you're fortunate, you'll be hired by a Wall Street firm that has a hedge fund or private equity arm—if you have a chance to be an analyst for something along these lines, grab it. It'll prepare you well for work at the top private equity firms down the road. If your forte is research, then the sell-side research arms will give you a good start, especially as many firms now seek to not only issue "buy" and "sell" ratings, but also to identify potential takeover targets for an arbitrage-hungry investment community.

If your background and interest lies in the field of operations, you'll have plenty of chances to prove yourself to private equity firms. Your undergrad or MBA degree will make you attractive to a wide variety of public and private corporations. Make a name for yourself as a cost-cutter, someone who can wring efficiency out of any situation, a streamliner and a value-finder. A series of increasingly responsible and successful positions, with the proven ability to find value and cut costs, will ultimately make private equity firms take notice, though you will need years of experience in that kind of role. That is, of course, unless you happen to be working for a company that's bought by a private equity firm. In that case, you could find yourself rising

Visit the Vault Finance Career Channel at **www.vault.com/finance** - with insider firm profiles, message boards, the Vault Finance Job Board and more.

VAULT CAREER LIBRARY

55

through the ranks quickly, and brought into the firm's other portfolio companies to work your magic.

Bringing your experience to the table

You could also find yourself primed for a private equity career after time in the legal or accounting fields. Major law firms like Skadden Arps and Vedder Price are known for their work advising private equity firms on their deals. The law, of course, is a completely different career path, and one beyond the scope of this book, but a strong background in contract law and corporate law could prime you for a very lucrative position—either advising private equity firms or serving as in-house counsel to some of the bigger ones.

Likewise, Ernst & Young, PricewaterhouseCooper and other major accounting firms have a strong private equity practice. Their accountants and actuaries investigate and certify the records of potential takeover targets, and also help determine whether a given private equity firm can leverage up safely to take over a company. They provide an important reality check on the private equity firms' earnings and cost-savings projections as well.

How I Got My Job: From Investment Banking to Private Equity

Joe, 39, New York

Everybody thought I was going to be a "lifer." I started at my firm right out of college as an analyst with asset management. I eventually moved into investment banking, the M&A advisory business, and it just clicked, and I took off. Pretty soon, I was a VP and second in command on a bunch of really great deals.

Then one day my MD up and left the company after, like, 30 years or something, and heads off to a private equity firm. Two weeks didn't go by before he called me, wanting me to come with him. I headed over there to talk about it, and I was just impressed. It really is the top of the mountain when it comes to deal-making. I've been at the private equity firm for about five years now, and just made MD myself.

Job Hunting and Networking

There are a few sites, such as the Private Equity Search Digest (www.jobsearchdigest.com/pesd), that feature jobs posted by private equity firms. Almost universally, the jobs are with small firms seeking to make names for themselves, and the sites feature a great deal of venture capital positions as well. These aren't necessarily bad things, of course, and plenty of top private equity people got their start at smaller firms. But if you're looking for an entry point into a top-notch firm, this is about 10 steps back.

The real key to finding a great job in private equity is networking. The so-called "old boys' network" is alive and well throughout private equity, and who you know will get you in the door for at least an informational interview. Start with your college's or MBA program's alumni office. The schools love it when they're known for producing top talent, so they're very eager to help put you in contact with alumni willing to help you. Most MBA programs have at least one or two alumni working in the field, and the top programs will give you the pick of the bunch. When reaching out to these people, be polite and courteous, and recognize they're doing **you** a favor by even responding to your e-mail. Don't rattle off a list of accomplishments when a handful will do. Keep it short and polite. And follow your school's lead, too—if they give you an e-mail, use it. Don't call the firm and ask for the person. If they wanted to be reached via phone, you would've been given a number.

Networking strategies

Professional societies and school clubs are also a good tool for networking. Whatever your specialty, there's a society or association that can help you. Minority organizations are particularly helpful, as part of the society's overall mission is to get more minorities working on Wall Street. Again, be respectful and polite, and don't waste anybody's time.

These strategies are good even if you're well beyond your school years. But if you're already working in the financial industry, you've got a leg up on everyone else. Chances are you've had contact with someone in your firm who's had contact with private equity firms. Put your feelers out among your colleagues and see what happens. Be discreet, of course, unless you don't mind your current boss knowing that you're looking for a change. In some companies, going to your boss is actually the thing to do, since some bosses are good at networking on your behalf. But that's a judgment call you'll have to make based on your individual situation.

Visit the Vault Finance Career Channel at **www.vault.com/finance** - with insider
firm profiles, message boards, the Vault Finance Job Board and more.

VAULT CAREER LIBRARY   57

Finally, keep good notes and records of people you've met through the financial world. Get business cards, send thank-you e-mails and do your best to keep in touch—without being a pest. For someone you've met at a conference, for example, and haven't seen since, an e-mail every six months or so is a good way to say hello and keep the relationship going. For folks you've seen a little more regularly, a friendly e-mail once a quarter is effective. Any more than that, you're probably dealing with them enough to not need a "remember me?" e-mail. Keep track of their movements throughout Wall Street, update them briefly on what you've been up to, and be sure to be helpful when you can. It seems like a lot of work, but done right, you'll eventually know someone who knows someone who might have the ear of a Henry Kravis or Stephen Schwarzman. And that could lead to a job in private equity down the road.

How I Got My Job: The Turnaround Specialist

Michael, 52, Connecticut

I spent 20 years in a Fortune 100 company, rising to the level of executive vice president in charge of a succession of divisions. During that time, of course, I had the opportunity to revamp those divisions. Pretty soon, I was being moved internally from place to place, as kind of the fix-it man. But after a while, it got a little boring and a little repetitive. The company was in good shape.

I've kept in touch with a college classmate through the years, and he's at a private equity firm that just bought a really troubled company. I figured why not, I'll give him a call. We had a great chat, and followed up a week later at his office. I came on about seven years ago, and have been at three portfolio companies in one capacity or another. They have real problems, real operational messes, and I really enjoy going in and fixing them. It's the challenge that I missed, and I'm getting it here.

The Interview

CHAPTER 6

The interview is perhaps the most important part of the whole employment process. If you've gotten that far, it's obvious to the firm that, on paper, you're a viable candidate. This is your opportunity to stand out from that resume, and the resumes of everyone else who's applied.

Things to remember

There are a handful of mistakes that, firms say, candidates make in their interviews. The first is projecting the kind of hot-shot aggressiveness that seems to be the Wall Street stereotype. That may be all well and good for a position on a trading desk, but private equity firms tend to prefer more cerebral, thoughtful candidates. Their investments are for the long haul, and they don't invest lightly. Be strong and stick to your convictions, but don't be cocky. Present yourself as an aggressive value seeker, but one who does his or her homework.

Secondly, remember who you'd be working for—the private equity fund's shareholders and the firm itself, not the portfolio company. "The industry has a sort of PR campaign going that says we're good for companies," says one managing director of a small private equity firm. "We present ourselves as a hope for troubled companies, someone they can turn to. That's all well and good, and it's often true, but we're there to find value and make money. Period." So don't make the mistake of putting a target or portfolio company's interests ahead of the fund's or firm's. Especially with hypothetical questions, you need to at least discuss the various value opportunities in dismantling a portfolio company's unprofitable divisions, spinning off pieces, or just closing up the whole company and selling the real estate it has for a profit.

Questions during an interview with a private equity firm tend to fall into four categories—your expertise, your knowledge, your character, and your vision and goals. The following are some samples of each.

Visit the Vault **Finance** Career Channel at **www.vault.com/finance**—with insider firm profiles, message boards, the Vault Finance Job Board and more.

VAULT CAREER LIBRARY   59

Sample Expertise Questions

Tell me what you did in your last position that helped your company find value?

This goes to the very core of what it means to work for a private equity firm. You should be able to walk into an interview with four to five solid examples of how your actions directly saved your previous employers money. This could be from developing operational efficiencies to ferreting out information that helped save money on an M&A deal. Maybe your research helped a company develop a new product line, or your ideas spurred cost savings on benefits. Whatever it is, be prepared to talk frankly and in detail about how you are an agent of value creation.

What are you most proud of in your career to date?

This is another opportunity to talk about things you've done to help create value. It can be an investment you identified or a trend you spotted, or any of the things mentioned above. But make it a good one, and make it relevant to the private equity firm's goals.

What's been the most disappointing thing you've experienced in your career so far?

This is a very nice way of asking if you've learned from your mistakes. Nobody's going to get it right all the time, and they're going to want to know how you deal with adversity. Now, if your actions directly resulted in torpedoing a billion-dollar M&A deal … perhaps you may not want to mention that! But be prepared to talk about a project or deal that didn't go as planned. Don't blame others too much, either. Take responsibility for your part and explain how you've changed your approach since. Come off as having learned something from the experience.

Sample Knowledge Questions

What do you think is going to happen to LBOs/M&A/private equity in the coming months and years?

As we've discussed already, the private equity industry is going through a difficult transition period. You need to be up to speed on the state of major deals out there, financing, future growth, fund raising, the whole thing. Don't be surprised if a piece in *The Wall Street Journal* or *The Daily Deal* from that very morning is mentioned, and be prepared to respond to it. Naturally, a reasonably bullish outlook for the industry is likely an asset—why else are you applying?—but don't sugarcoat it, either. Talk about the challenges facing the industry in a reasonable way, how the industry might overcome them, and why you ultimately think the industry will continue to grow and prosper.

Is the market for mega-cap M&A/LBO deals done?

Another question having to do with your knowledge of current events. There was a point when the industry seemed to be poised for that $100 billion LBO deal. That may no longer be the case, at least over the next few years. Do your homework, read up on everything you can and talk to contacts in the industry. Get a feel for the trends within private equity, and be able to talk intelligently about them.

Company X is a struggling retailer with prime real estate. Do you break it up and sell the land, or try to refresh the business?

You can expect at least one hypothetical question regarding your area of expertise during the interview, and probably another that has more focus and better elucidation than the one above. Know enough about the industry to mention a previous deal involving a similar situation and how you might handle things now.

Sample Personality Questions

What makes a good private equity deal-maker/fundraiser/researcher/ associate?

This should be relatively easy. For most positions, it's someone with an eye for opportunities to create value, developing plans to create value, executing said plans, etc. The whole point of a private equity firm is to wring as much value as one can out of an investment. And that should be the focus of your answer.

Why do you want to work in private equity?

Money, prestige or a perception of the industry as the "next big thing" will get you shown the door. Of course, those already working in private equity would be lying if they said they didn't enjoy those things. But ultimately, once the money's in the bank and the person's name is in boldface in the newspaper, the challenge is what keeps them coming back. Private equity, to those in the industry, represents the very pinnacle of investing. Turning

Visit the Vault Finance Career Channel at **www.vault.com/finance**—with insider firm profiles, message boards, the Vault Finance Job Board and more.

VAULT CAREER LIBRARY   **61**

around whole companies, finding value where there doesn't appear to be any … these are what keeps private equity folks in the game.

Alternatively, you'll sometimes be asked why *this* firm. Know the firm, and know what makes it tick. Tailor your answer accordingly.

Where do you want to be in five years?

If you're young and going after the equivalent of an analyst or associate position, feel free to talk about other opportunities. Perhaps you want to get an MBA if you don't have one already, or even a doctorate. Perhaps you want to build on your experience and join a portfolio company. It's good to have other ideas, but make sure that your position in private equity takes priority. It's perfectly fine to say, "I don't know, but I'm eager to find out what kind of opportunities would present themselves if I get the chance to work here." If you're older and applying for an experienced associate, VP or managing director position, the firm isn't going to want to hear anything other than a commitment to staying and growing with the firm. They're potentially going to throw a lot of money at you, so reassure them that their return on investment will last a good long while.

Sample Vision Questions

What do you think this company does right, and what do you think we do wrong?

First off, a bit of a trick question here. The company doesn't do anything wrong, it simply has areas in which it can improve. That said, you should be knowledgeable enough about the company and its recent deals to talk intelligently about how the company operates. Play up its strengths, certainly, but don't be sycophantic. And don't pull any punches on ways it can improve, but again, don't be too negative.

Where are the next opportunities for private equity?

The answer to this depends on the position, of course. If you're interested in fund raising, talk about new potential sources of funds, including any ideas floating around about public offerings and the like, or potential new sources of private placements. If you're in deal-making or operations, be ready to discuss the trends you've read about recently, such as emerging market LBOs or a particular domestic sector. New financing plans are always welcome, too.

If you were given a chance to go after Company Y, would you take it, and what would you do with it?

Another hypothetical, with "company Y" likely a company in the news lately for various and sundry problems. If it's a company with too much debt and not enough upside, feel free to say you wouldn't take it. If it's a company with a decent balance sheet and some operational problems, then talk about what you'd do. Ultimately, you'd have to be up on the news to consider whether there's an opportunity to create value within the framework of an acquisition.

Your Turn: Questions You Should Ask

You should always walk in armed with questions about the company so that you can glean more information about your potential employer and they can come away with some appreciation that you've done your homework. That said, this won't be the time to ask about benefits and pay—ask too early and you look greedy. Greed is good, but there's a time and a place, and your initial interviewing at a firm isn't the time, unless the subject is broached first.

Instead, you want to ask smart questions about the company to learn more about how it does its business—and show that you know your stuff as well.

Roughly, how many people do you hire each year? What's the turnover like here?

This is a good basic question for any company, let alone one in private equity. This question gives you a sense of the rarity of openings, as well as how long people stay at the company. The demand for good private equity employees is strong, and anybody with private equity experience can go elsewhere for more money, so don't get too alarmed if turnover seems a little higher than you might expect. That said, low turnover is a very good sign—people are making plenty of money, and the work keeps them interested and fulfilled.

How do you deal with the issue of employee retention?

Following the previous question, this is the sneaky way of asking about pay and benefits without actually asking. You're likely to start a conversation about "aligning the interests of the company and employee" through various bonus programs and the like. You may also get a sense of the company's culture, especially if they actually bring up things like work environment, corporate values and work/life balance. (Admittedly, work/life balance discussions will be rare—you won't be expected to have a life.) Be wary of

Visit the Vault Finance Career Channel at **www.vault.com/finance**—with insider firm profiles, message boards, the Vault Finance Job Board and more.

VAULT CAREER LIBRARY   **63**

the interviewer who says he or she isn't worried; every firm on Wall Street should be. Even after the rough end to 2007, there's plenty of demand for top talent throughout high finance, and private equity firms are still up against tough competition from hedge funds, on the riskier side, and from more traditional Wall Street firms that may now be more averse to risk. You want to hear reassurance that this is a top priority for the firm.

How much do you plan to take advantage of the recent interest in private equity investing to grow the business?

Knowing the current mindset of private equity fund investors and the ebb and flow of the business is important, and this question shows you have some interest in that. This will also give you a sense of the strength of the company's business and its future plans for expansion.

In your acquisition of Company X, you opted for Exit Strategy A instead of Exit Strategy B. Why is that?

Asking smart questions about recent or historical acquisitions is always a nice way to show off your research and intelligence, and also get a better sense of the company's investing philosophy. That said, the key word here is *smart*. If you're going to ask about any deals, know them cold, and ask specific questions. "Were you happy with the way Deal Y turned out?" is not going to make you look good, and the interviewer is going to sit back and say, "Well, sure." But if you can ask a smart question about the financing structure of Deal Y, that will get your interviewer talking.

ON THE JOB

Life as a Private Equity Specialist

CHAPTER 7

Once you've landed a job with a private equity firm, you can expect some of the most interesting, fast-paced work on Wall Street. The pay and benefits will be commensurate with this kind of work—but so will the pressure and the hours.

Lifestyle

"Whatever job you take on Wall Street, you aren't doing it because you like your weekends free." Those are the very canny words of a major investment banking CEO, and they especially hold true for those working in private equity. Your hours will be long, and you will be one of those people deftly wielding a BlackBerry at soccer games, in the corners of restaurants or even poolside. These are high-stakes investments, after all, and if you're helping to manage a billion-dollar stake in a major company, you'll be held responsible for the outcome.

Entry-level lifestyles

At the analyst and associate levels, or in any support role, you can expect long hours—8 a.m. to 7 p.m. wouldn't be seen as onerous. But on the other hand, unless there's something big pending, your weekends and vacation time can be your own. That said, if you're supporting the deal-makers, and they're deep in negotiations with a major publicly traded company, you'll be expected to be right there with them on a Saturday night at 10:30 p.m.

Executive lifestyles

In more senior positions, your day-to-day hours can actually be much more reasonable—8:30 a.m. to 6 p.m. in some cases—but you'll also find the line between work and the rest of your life to blur considerably. Some of your meals will be spent working, while evening conference calls and the occasional late-night panic e-mail will eat into what you once may have considered your private life. Travel will pick up considerably as well, no matter your role. You may have to fly out to Sacramento to convince CalPERS to invest in your fund, or head to Atlanta to finish a buyout deal, or tour a portfolio company's facility in China looking for ways to improve productivity and cut costs.

It's not like you won't be able to take vacations, but since you'll still be held responsible for outcomes in your absence, most high-level workers in private equity tend to schedule vacations carefully. If you're in major negotiations for a deal right around Christmas, you may not be able to get away for the holiday. And you'd be wise to schedule your summer trip *after* your portfolio company's annual report to the fund's board of directors.

For most high-level private equity employees, this lifestyle is par for the course. And if you've worked on Wall Street in other capacities, you're likely used to the trade-off. But if you're just starting out and are eying a private equity career, bear it mind that your career can quickly become its own lifestyle—especially if you're successful!

Pay and Benefits

With billions of dollars at stake in each transaction, private equity firms are more than willing to pay for talent—so long as that talent executes properly. You can generally expect salaries, bonuses and benefits to be at the high end of Wall Street pay scales. It's not quite what hedge fund managers make, but it's generally on par with the top investment banking salaries.

In the few entry-level positions available at private equity firms, you can expect to make a base salary of $60,000 to $75,000 as an undergraduate degree holder, and roughly $125,000 as a newly minted MBA holder. There are bonuses on top of that, as well. Some firms have separate personal and companywide bonuses, while others combine them into one bonus. Typically, in your first few years you can earn 25 to 35 percent of your base salary in bonus money.

Once you've grown out of these support roles, or if you're coming into a private equity firm with more experience, the base salary grows geometrically while your bonus money grows exponentially. Those who are in direct-action or supervisory roles can expect base salaries ranging from $250,000 to $1 million or more, depending on how closely they work with fund investors, deal-makers or the portfolio companies. Their bonuses depend greatly on how well they manage their work. Did the deal-maker get the best terms for the fund? Did the fund raiser bring above-quota money into the fund for the year? Did the portfolio company manager cut costs and boost margins above projections? The bonus money for private equity professionals at the vice president, principal or managing director levels can be anywhere from two to 10 times their base salaries.

Big benefits

And of course, like most Wall Street firms, private equity employers generally don't skimp on other benefits. Medical, dental and various insurance plans are generally very good. Some firms will also set aside up to 20 percent of base salary in a retirement fund—that's on top of the base salary, not a cut into it. The retirement fund can, in many cases, be invested in the company's private equity funds, giving workers an additional stake in their company's success. Indeed, it's worth noting that at the managing director level, most companies will take a cut of your bonus money and roll it into the fund for you. Given the outsized returns and personal stake in the firm's success, few complain.

Opportunities for Advancement

Most private equity firms are very tight-knit groups—note that even Blackstone has just 400 employees worldwide. It would seem, then, that the opportunities for advancement in a given private equity company would be limited. But, actually, the opposite is true. Once you get in the door, private equity companies can be surprising meritocracies. Almost universally, there are no set number of managing directors at a company, no "slots" for position and promotion. Do good work, and you'll get bumped up in title, pay and responsibility.

If you're starting in a support role, you'll likely be assigned to a handful of high-level staff. You can quickly become the "go-to" person for top managers if you can tackle your assignments with enthusiasm, accuracy and speed. In turn, you'll make your managers look good. A few firms promote this kind of relationship through mentor training and the like, but for the most part, you should seek to develop a strong working relationship with your supervisor and manager. As you both succeed, he or she can take you with them to more and greater responsibility.

It all depends on you

Once you've graduated from support roles, your opportunities for advancement really depend solely on your performance. The private equity company's top management will have very specific goals in mind for everything you might do—dollar amounts for funds to be raised, financing terms for a bond issuance or line of credit, total dollar value of a deal or total amount in cost savings in the first year after an acquisition. The targets, for

Visit the Vault Finance Career Channel at **www.vault.com/finance**—with insider firm profiles, message boards, the Vault Consulting Job Board and more.

VAULT CAREER LIBRARY   **69**

the most part, aren't overly ambitious, though to be fair, you'll have to work hard just to meet them. And the expectation is that, unless something unexpected happens, you will exceed them.

If you can do that, then you'll be on your way. Again, there's no set number of managing directors at any given firm, so if you're a canny deal-maker or particularly adept at finding and fixing operational weaknesses in portfolio companies, you'll be called upon to do it again. And again. But performance is absolutely critical. You certainly will experience a setback or two, but you'll also be measured by how quickly you overcome it—and by how much.

Day in the Life: Entry-Level

Eric, 26, is an associate at a midsized private equity firm in Manhattan.

6:30 a.m.: I'm already up and dressed and heading out the door to catch a cab. I'm lucky enough to be making enough already to afford a cab to work every day after three years, and I only have to walk a half-block to find one.

7:15 a.m.: In the door at work, a cup of Starbucks in hand. I've responded to the most urgent e-mails on the BlackBerry on the ride down, so at this point, I'm taking on the less urgent or more complicated things that have to be done before the principal gets in at 8. Some of these are research items that I'll have to get to later, others can be answered pretty easily.

8:15 a.m.: Meet briefly with my principal to see where the day will take us. In general, we're working on two or three different things at once. Right now, we're in the middle of negotiations with one company, looking at distressed debt at another and in preliminary research on a third. I'm given some research to do and some calls to make for the day.

9:00 a.m.: A quick chat with my opposite at the investment bank that's advising on one of our deals. We handle the grunt stuff so the managing directors and such can do their thing. In this case, we're trying to get details on possible debt structures to do after the deal, to see what both sides can stomach.

10:00 a.m.: I spend the next couple of hours digging up some distressed debt historicals and putting together a profile of our distressed debt idea. I'm starting to wonder whether it's going to be worth it.

12:00 p.m.: Lunch. Au Bon Pain today. I take it back to my desk and keep going.

1:00 p.m.: The investment bank calls back, and it looks like we may have some movement on structuring future debt at the company that's furthest along in negotiations. I give my principal the heads up and we set up a call between their investment bank, our investment bank, us and the company. We manage to do it for 5—pretty fast.

2:00 p.m.: Prep for the conference call. We gather all the material we have, call and e-mail back and forth, and get a basic agenda ginned up for everyone to see. I give my principal a "to-do" list of things left outstanding. I also order up some dinner for everyone in our office who will be on the call.

5:00 p.m.: We start the call and start hashing out the debt structures. If I have ideas, I pass notes to my principal.

6:00 p.m.: Dinner arrives. We keep going on the call as we eat.

7:20 p.m.: The call wraps up. There's a preliminary agreement, but both sides have to go back and run it up the flagpole. I head back to my desk to enter my new tasks into my Outlook before I head home. That'll include the flagpole document—I bullet out what should go in there and give it to my principal before I head home.

8:00 p.m.: Cab back home. I may work a little after dinner, or not. This was a long day—usually I'm out by 6.

Day in the Life: Researcher

7:00 a.m.: Get on the train and head into the city with a sheaf of research notes from the night before.

8:00 a.m.: Arrive at work. If it's Monday, prepare for the weekly meeting. "The Monday meeting tends to last most of the day. Everyone talks about everything the company's doing, the state of every investment or potential target. And everyone chips in. People come in and out as needed, but for the executive committee, it's a 9-to-5 thing." Since it's not Monday, gather the latest research from Wall Street on potential takeover targets.

9:00 a.m.: Present updates, if needed, to the executive committee on previously discussed targets. Generally done through e-mail.

9:30 a.m.: Hit the phones. There's always more to find out beyond what you read in the papers or in the research notes. I'll call clients, suppliers, anybody that the target deals with to see how they do things and what their problems might be.

Visit the Vault Finance Career Channel at **www.vault.com/finance**—with insider firm profiles, message boards, the Vault Consulting Job Board and more.

VAULT CAREER LIBRARY   **71**

11:00 a.m.: Previously scheduled interview with a representative of a target company. This is purely informational, and both our guys and their guys know we're doing it. We're just saying we want a stake, they're saying they don't want to sell, but that's how the dance begins. So we meet and get a sense of each other at a lower level before we hand it off to the managing directors and the C-level executives.

12:00 p.m.: Lunch, target company rep in tow.

1:30 p.m.: Back in the office, writing up the report on the meeting along with potential follow-up questions and research.

2:00 p.m.: More phone work and computer research.

3:30 p.m.: Meeting with the deal team on a current negotiation. They seem to think they're overpaying, and they want us to take a look at a piece of the target's business again. Turns out we hadn't revisited the topic in a few months, and it was easy to find out what was going on. Probably saved a few million there.

5:00 p.m.: Conference call with portfolio company managers about the latest in supply chain research.

6:00 p.m.: Order dinner while going over the day's activity on portfolio and target companies. Write up developments for directors as needed.

8:00 p.m.: Home.

Day in the Life: Fund Raiser and Investor Relations

8:00 a.m.: Arrive at work. I'm lucky in that my position doesn't require a lot of overnight work. My morning is my own. Sometimes I even hit the gym before I get in, though not as much as I should. I answer e-mails, some from fund holders with questions about recent news reports on private equity. Dig up the latest information on a fund for a status call.

9:00 a.m.: Status call with major investor. This is a major state pension fund that placed a good chunk of money with us. So we give them an update every so often, anywhere from every other week to once a quarter, depending on what they want and need.

10:00 a.m.: Grab a cab and head across town for a sales meeting.

10:30 a.m.: Sales meeting. A major university is considering a placement with us. It's my job to show them what we've done, what our plans are, and the mechanics of making the placement. In this case, they're interested but want a follow-up meeting with their chancellor and our bosses. So on the ride back to the office, I'm on the BlackBerry to see which of the bosses would be available and when.

12:00 p.m.: Following up on a lead. Even private equity firms cold call sometimes. A friend introduced me to a private banker a few weeks ago, and I'm following up to see if there's a chance to do something together.

1:00 p.m.: Lunch. I always try to get out of the office for at least a half hour. Not everybody has that luxury.

1:30 p.m.: Another status call with an investor.

2:30 p.m.: Reviewing the quarterly letter to investors. It's early yet, but you want to be out there in front of them, whatever the news, so you can own the message.

3:00 p.m.: Meeting to go over the quarterly letter to investors with the writers and marketing consultant.

4:00 p.m.: Preparing for another sales call, this one for a hedge fund. You target your message differently. I wouldn't make the same arguments for a university that I would for a hedge fund.

4:30 p.m.: Catching the train out to Connecticut with a VP who helps run the fund.

6:00 p.m.: Dinner meeting with the hedge fund. When the VP is there, I tend to let her do a lot of the talking, especially when they get down and dirty with the numbers. I simply keep things moving and make sure we tackle all the high points.

9:00 p.m.: Back to the train station and into the city en route to home, with BlackBerry messages going the entire trip.

Visit the Vault Finance Career Channel at **www.vault.com**finance - with insider firm profiles, message boards, the Vault Consulting Job Board and more.

VAULT CAREER LIBRARY   **73**

Day in the Life: Deal-Maker

6:00 a.m.: Up and reading the presentation books drawn up by the associates the night before. Phone calls to the associates ("to wake them up") to get some changes going before the day's meetings begin.

7:30 a.m.: Picked up by the car. More e-mails and phone calls.

8:30 a.m.: At the office. Check in with the managing director for an update of the previous day's negotiations and what's planned for today.

9:00 a.m.: Meeting with the team. We'll have the updates in the presentation book done, we'll have a strategy mapped out. This is simply kind of a double check before we head over.

9:40 a.m.: In the cars and heading to the investment bank. We have a war room set up there, too, but we're only 15 minutes away, so we do a lot of work back at the office.

10:00 a.m.: First negotiating session. The target company always tends to come up with a new wrinkle overnight, as do we. So we spend the first few hours going through those. Sometimes we can just call each other on our B.S. and move on, but sometimes we have to retrench and figure out what they're saying.

12:30 p.m.: Break for lunch. Hit the phones to figure out countermoves based on the morning's presentations.

1:30 p.m.: The real session. This is where stuff gets done. Today we drilled down and agreed upon a value for their major business arm, which was key. We got a lot more than they did out of it.

6:00 p.m.: Have dinner sent over. Informal chatting between the two sides over dinner.

7:00 p.m.: Wrap up the day's talks.

7:30 p.m.: Convene with the team in the war room and dole out assignments for the overnight. Make a few phone calls to key people and update the MD again.

9:00 p.m.: Call the car and go home.

Day in the Life: Portfolio Company Manager

6:30 a.m.: Conference call from home with a European shareholder. I don't do a lot of shareholder relations, but they'll occasionally pull me in if a shareholder has a specific question about a portfolio company's prospects. They had some concerns about something they read in the local press there. I hate the British tabloids.

7:45 a.m.: Ride into work, checking e-mail the whole way.

8:30 a.m.: At work and responding to e-mails. I'll read them in the car, but I hate typing on a phone. Most of my overnight stuff is status reports anyway, and they don't need too much help from me.

9:00 a.m.: Conference call with the management team at a portfolio company. This is a weekly thing at most portfolio companies. We go over their numbers and their goals, and see how they're doing. I make suggestions on improving things or approaches to take. This is a pretty short one. We do a longer monthly one and go out once a quarter for a big sit-down.

10:30 a.m.: Meeting with a potential hire. I'm always on the lookout for good turnaround guys.

11:00 a.m.: Car to the airport. I'm heading out to Cleveland for a big quarterly meeting with another portfolio company. I'm on the road maybe twice a month for various things.

1:30-3:30 p.m.: In the air. I'd like to be saying that I'm reading a book or napping, but I'm going over the company's performance and calling out questions I need to ask.

4:00 p.m.: Car to the company headquarters. Settling in and getting prepared for the rest of the visit.

6:00 p.m.: Dinner in the company boardroom with the executive team. This is sort of the informal meeting before the real meeting the following day with the (private equity) firm's top brass on the phone. I tend not to ask too many questions here. I want to hear from them how things are going. I'll pipe up on a few things, but this is their chance to vent at me.

9:00 p.m.: At the hotel and out cold within an hour.

Visit the Vault Finance Career Channel at **www.vault.com/finance** - with insider firm profiles, message boards, the Vault Consulting Job Board and more.

V∧ULT CAREER LIBRARY   **75**

Private Equity Career Paths

CHAPTER 8

There's more to life than deal-making at private equity firms. There are numerous career paths you can choose upon entering the field, and even more should you decide to leave. If you perform well, the vast majority of your options will be fulfilling and lucrative.

The Typical Career Path

Hopefully by now you realize there's nothing truly typical about working for private equity firms—they're some of the most dynamic companies on Wall Street. And the experiences you'll receive in working for one can rarely be duplicated anywhere else.

Breaking into the industry

There's no one single path into a private equity career. As we noted earlier, the top firms are starting to recruit at the graduate and undergraduate levels. But there are other avenues to explore. If you're an experienced hand at investor relations, for example, you could become a welcome addition to a private equity company's fund-raising and investor relations team. A whiz at financing could easily help a firm obtain credit for a buyout or to raise expansion capital for a portfolio company. And anyone working at a top Wall Street investment bank could well find a place in the deal making division of a private equity firm.

But you may not need a Wall Street pedigree, either. "I was a deputy comptroller at a portfolio company when they found me," says one top operational consultant for a private equity firm. "I had all these ideas my company considered, but when the buyout came, I had it all in writing and went to the new bosses. I ended up as CFO by the time we were IPO'ed four years later, and then went to work for them fixing other companies."

You may not even find yourself with an office at the private equity company, yet you'll be working for them over and over again. These companies are very adept at finding top talent within the ranks of portfolio companies. And these individuals may be called upon to take similar roles at new portfolio companies to work their magic again and again. At the most extreme, some private equity companies have their own preferred chief executives, like Bob Nardelli, one-time Home Depot CEO, who now holds the same title at the

Visit the Vault Finance Career Channel at **www.vault.com/finance**—with insider firm profiles, message boards, the Vault Consulting Job Board and more.

VAULT CAREER LIBRARY 77

Chrysler Group thanks to old friends at Cerberus who were impressed with his ability to contain costs throughout this career.

Within the Private Equity Firm

Once you're working at a private equity firm, despite the general mobility and performance-based atmosphere of most private equity firms, moving to new positions within the company can be difficult, and cross-pollination between divisions is rare. The skills needed to raise money from institutional investors and those needed to obtain the best financing aren't dissimilar, but they require training. Likewise, it can be one thing to identify operational weaknesses within a target company and quite another to implement solutions.

Who's at the top?

The top management of most private equity firms come from the ranks of those who can identify potential deals, and then close said deals. Fund raisers are important, but ultimately don't have the know-how to spot great investments. Likewise, operations experts can take what they're given and improve upon it, but are very much used to getting things done with the full authority of management behind them, rather than through delicate negotiation.

That's not to say that the deal-makers rule the roost entirely. As we've seen, the top people in each of the firm's divisions have to sign off on any given investment. But so much hinges on the firm's ability to identify the best investments and get them on board, so it's no surprise that people like Henry Kravis or Stephen Schwarzman are deal-makers first and foremost.

Exceptions to the rule

That's not to say there isn't *any* cross-training. Kravis and Schwarzman are deal-makers, of course, but even they will make time to schmooze with an institution pondering a billion-dollar investment with the firm. An operations expert may be called upon to have input on any given deal negotiations. And a fund raiser and financier may work together to ensure the company can put enough money together in enough time for a deal to work. But generally, everyone has a role and a job to do—most of these firms are too small to dedicate the time necessary to cross-train any but their top employees.

Yet, as mentioned above, you can become one of those top employees—all you have to do is execute well, over time, on everything you're given. A challenge, but one that most attracted to this industry should welcome.

Leaving the Private Equity Firm

There are downsides to working for private equity firms that, in time, can prove to be difficult to live with. For one, because they're small, you may find yourself taking on the same responsibilities over and over again. Yes, they're responsibilities worth millions, but they can also be repetitive. And the guys sitting at the very apex of the firm aren't going anywhere—their name is figuratively, if not literally, on the door of the company. And you may also decide that the breakneck pace and crisis management required of many private equity employees has worn thin. Even the most jaded Wall Street operator will cop to wanting to spend more time with his or her family after a while.

Where do we go from here?

Thankfully, the rest of the financial sector welcomes people with private equity experience with open arms. Knowing how choosy private equity firms are, and the kind of responsibilities their employees work with, the rest of Wall Street is happy to get their hands on someone with advanced experience at a firm like Blackstone, Cerberus or KKR. Indeed, you may have already made plenty of contacts through your private equity work to make a transition easy.

If you're involved in fund raising and investor relations, you have plenty of opportunities to "jump the fence" and go to work for those you sought money from. Major pension funds and Wall Street firms need someone who can assess past performance of a private equity fund before making an investment. If you've made the case successfully in the past, you know what to look for in a private equity investment and can help decide what's best for your new company. Alternatively, having dealt with major investors in the past, most other Wall Street firms dealing with big-money institutional investors may want to put your expertise to work on their clients as well. In these cases, you'll have more support staff behind you to make sure you're getting the work done, though admittedly the pay not be as stratospheric.

If you've worked to identify investments, the possibilities are far broader. Hedge funds, especially those who have recently made their own private

Visit the Vault Finance Career Channel at **www.vault.com/finance**—with insider firm profiles, message boards, the Vault Consulting Job Board and more.

VAULT CAREER LIBRARY   **79**

equity investments, need people like you to help identify their opportunities. Indeed, the hedge fund may not even want to buy the company outright, but could instead use your expertise to find companies *likely* to be bought out so they can buy up the stock and bet on which one will go private first. Individual companies of all stripes could also use you to help them figure out their own shortcomings and opportunities, while investment banks like Morgan Stanley and Merrill Lynch could use the same expertise for the benefit of their traditional M&A clients.

Deal-makers, of course, will always find a home on Wall Street, especially if they've closed some successful private equity buyouts. Most private equity deal-makers have already had plenty of contact with their counterparts at most major investment banks; they're the ones who negotiate on behalf of the companies being bought out. And a solid track record of deal-making could help you beyond M&A as well, as some multinational corporations have the need for an experienced negotiator and deal-maker for everything from government contracts to labor disputes.

Operational turnaround specialists, likewise, have few problems leaving private equity firms to work elsewhere. Just think of where Bob Nardelli might go next if he manages to turn Chrysler around without too many problems. Once disgraced for taking major pay packages at Home Depot while the stock price foundered, Nardelli is getting a huge second chance with Chrysler. A difficult chance, to be sure, but if he pulls it off, nobody will blanch at paying him to run another company down the road. This is an extreme example, of course, but if you had a hand in turning around a major company, your expertise will be in demand elsewhere. Indeed, you may find yourself courted by public companies who want the turnaround expertise— but don't want to be taken private! If you're interested, you can start talking to them. If not, you can just call the guy down the hall and clue him in on a potential takeover target.

Finally, those experts who can get major banks to extend credit or underwrite debt offerings have perhaps the most flexible post-private equity career paths. Everybody needs money, and if you have a deft touch with those who give it out, you'll find a home no matter what.

But why would you want to leave anyway?

Of course, with all this said, few people within a given private equity firm leave in any given year. They generally enjoy not only the compensation, but the lifestyle in place at most firms, and find the idea of leaving boring. The

Masters of the Universe mentality is alive and well in private equity, though in 2007, it's at least a bit more muted and humble.

Continuing Education and Improvement

For the most part, private equity firms tend to hire the talents they need, rather than develop from within. Even if a particular deal requires specialized knowledge—the LBO of a pharmaceutical company could require pharmacological expertise the firm doesn't have—consultants can be easily hired. Thus, there generally isn't a call for major ongoing educational efforts at most firms.

But they do have the money, and if you can come up with a compelling argument, you can generally get the funds for the continuing education you feel you need. For the private equity firms that employ actuaries, for example, they'll typically sponsor the tests you need for fellowship in the major actuarial societies. Likewise, if you're about to embark on negotiations with a Japanese firm, a crash course in language and business culture is certainly available. (Or, again, it might be the right place to simply hire a consultant.)

If you're starting at the very lowest rung of the ladder at a private equity firm, it's unlikely that the company will sponsor you for your MBA—indeed, most firms require it from the outset, unless they have specific undergrad recruitment plans or you have extensive experience elsewhere. If you've done good work for the company, you may be able to take a leave, get an MBA, and come back to the firm.

All this said, private equity firms are joining the rest of Wall Street in struggling with a dwindling pool of talent. A year from now, things could be very different, as more firms decide to grow from within instead of competing with hedge funds and investment banks for developed talent. And each firm, of course, is different, and can change policies at the drop of a hat. When you're talking with a firm about employment, be sure to ask about the current policies on continuing education and career development.

Visit the Vault Finance Career Channel at **www.vault.com/finance**—with insider firm profiles, message boards, the Vault Consulting Job Board and more.

V**A**ULT CAREER LIBRARY   **81**

Final Analysis

The private equity space is undergoing immense change. Easy credit—a staple of the takeovers of the past decade—could be drying up. And the storied firms that blazed the trail for private equity investing in the 1970s, 1980s and 1990s are now up against stiff competition from investment banks and hedge funds.

But there will always be a need for private equity investing—and thus, private equity firms.

It's here to stay

Few other classes of investment can produce the kinds of returns that a well-run private equity fund can achieve. For institutional investors—especially those sick of underperforming hedge funds in 2006 and 2007—private equity investing can unlock double-digit returns that most other investments can't near. Private equity investing also remains less tied to the vagaries of the stock market, and thus provides strong returns over time that only the best bull markets can match.

And when it comes right down to it, a firm like Blackstone, KKR, Carlyle or Bain is just far better equipped—in money, experience and ambition—to make private equity investing work. Hedge funds may dabble, and money-center banks and investment banks may open and close divisions based on the fads of the market, but the private equity firm has remained steady through all kinds of market conditions, gathering experience and knowledge that can't be found by dilettante players.

And for the foreseeable future, there will always be companies open to a private buyout. If the demands on public companies were great during the bull market from 2003 to mid-2007, they are piling on even higher in today's tense market environment. Quarterly numbers must be met, and stock buybacks and dividends are critical—stocks have been pummeled for even the slightest hint of weakness in earnings, and buybacks and dividends have become appeasements to shareholders.

In addition, the requirements of Sarbanes-Oxley—the regulatory law put in place after the Enron and WorldCom debacles—have proven to be onerous for many companies. Even if Sarbanes-Oxley's requirements are relaxed, as many anticipate could happen in 2008, private equity buyouts will always be a good opportunity for publicly traded companies to reinvent themselves outside of the glare of the public shareholders' spotlight.

It's too early to say how the credit crunch of 2007 (and into 2008) will play out. Buyout announcements in the fourth quarter of 2007 were half that of the

Visit the Vault Finance Career Channel at **www.vault.com/finance**—with insider firm profiles, message boards, the Vault Consulting Job Board and more.

VAULT CAREER LIBRARY   83

previous quarter, even as the Federal Reserve started cutting overall interest rates. The rate cuts are nice, and ostensibly make credit cheaper for private equity borrowers. The problem, however, is that in the face of the subprime-fueled credit debacle, the major Wall Street banks are now very gunshy.

In fact, there's been talk that the major investment banks—some of whom, like Citigroup and Merrill Lynch, are under new leadership—may pull out of credit-dependent units entirely, either shutting them down or spinning them off into private entities to get the inherent risk of these businesses off their books. A wholesale departure out of private equity remains unlikely for most Wall Street firms—it's just too profitable in the long run. But if the big banks start pulling out of private equity, that could leave more market share for independent firms.

"This is one of those times where you wait and see," says one long-time private equity investor. "You keep looking for value, you run your companies as best you can, you assuage your investors and you wait until it gets better while the competition freaks out and drops the ball. It happened before, and it'll happen again, and those who stick to their guns will be stronger for it."

APPENDIX

Appendix

Helpful Web Sites

Private equity search digest - jobsearchdigest.com

Blogging Buyouts - www.bloggingbuyouts.com

Apax - www.apax.com/Apax_Private_Equity_Rankings_2007.pdf

Firm Web Sites

Apax Partners
www.apax.com/en/news/story_1723.html

Apollo Investment Corporation
www.apolloic.com/contactus.html

Bain Capital
www.baincapital.com/pages.asp?b=7;
www.baincapital.com/careers.asp?b=16&l=16

Blackstone
www.blackstone.com/news/default.asp

Carlyle Group
www.thecarlylegroup.com/eng/mediacontacts/l3-media2106.html

Cerberus
www.cerberuscapital.com/news_media_con.html

Clayton, Dubilier and Rice
www.cdr-inc.com/index_news.html

CVC Capital Partners
www.cvc.com/Content/En/OurLocations/LocationDetails.aspx?AID=5030

Fortress Investment Group
phx.corporate-ir.net/phoenix.zhtml?c=205346&p=irol-newsArticle&ID
=1016069&highlight=

J.C. Flowers & Co. LLP
investing.businessweek.com/research/stocks/private/snapshot.asp?privcapId
=1089967

Visit the Vault Finance Career Channel at **www.vault.com/**finance—with insider
firm profiles, message boards, the Vault Consulting Job Board and more.

VAULT CAREER LIBRARY 87

KKR
www.kkr.com/who/offices.html

Madison Dearborn Partners
www.mdcp.com/contact.asp

Permira (Europe)
www.permira.com/en/contacts/contacts.html

Providence Equity Partners
www.providenceequitypartners.com

Riverstone LLC
www.riverstonellc.com/contact_us/index.html

Silver Lake Partners
www.silverlake.com/content.php?page=news

Summit Partners
www.summitpartners.com/news/media_inquiries.aspx?mid=6&SID=605

Texas Pacific Group
www.texaspacificgroup.com/contact/index.html

Thomas Cressey Equity Partners
www.thomacressey.com/contact_us.php

Thomas H. Lee Partners
www.thlee.com

Warburg Pincus
www.warburgpincus.com/contact/index.html

Welsh, Carson, Anderson & Stowe
www.welshcarson.com

Recommended Reading

Anderson, Jenny, "The Old Money in Private Equity Isn't Ready to Welcome the New," *The New York Times*, July 20, 2007, pg. C5.

Bartlett, Sarah, *Money Machine: How KKR Manufactured Power and Profits*, Beard Books, 2005.

Bierman, Harold, *Private Equity: Transforming Public Stock to Create Value*, John Wiley & Sons, 2003.

Burrough and Helvar, *Barbarians at the Gate: The Fall of RJR Nabisco*, HarperCollins, paperback reprint 2003.

Conde Nast Portfolio—www.portfolio.com/news-markets/national-news/portfolio/2007/03/29/Whats-Wrong-With-This-Picture

De la Merced, Michael, "Wary Buyers May Scuttle Two Deals," *The New York Times*, Sept. 22, 2007, pg C1.

Goldstein, Matthew, "Hedge Funds Jump Into Private Equity," *BusinessWeek*, Feb. 26, 2007, pg. 46.

Krantz, Matt, "Private-equity firms put brakes on stock offerings," *USA Today*, Oct. 16, 2007, pg. 3B.

Lerner, Hardymon et. al., *Venture Capital and Private Equity*: *A Casebook, Third Edition*, John Wiley & Sons, 2004.

Lerner and Hardymon, *Venture Capital and Private Equity: A Casebook, Vol. 2*, John Wiley & Sons, 2001.

Povaly, Stefan, *Private Equity Exits: Divestment Process Management for Leveraged Buyouts*, Springer-Verlag, 2007.

Sorkin, Andrew Ross, "In Defense of Schwarzman," *The New York Times*, July 29, 2007, pg. BU6.

Sorkin and Merced, "Behind the Veil at Blackstone? Probably Another Veil," *The New York Times*, March 19, 2007, pg. C3.

Story, Louise, "Bye, Bye B-School," *The New York Times*, Sept. 16, 2007, Section 3, pg. 1.

Thornton, Emily, "Education of a Dealmaker: 'I Got Cocky,'" *BusinessWeek*, Sept. 17, 2007, pg. 48.

Visit the Vault Finance Career Channel at **www.vault.com**/finance—with insider firm profiles, message boards, the Vault Consulting Job Board and more.

VAULT CAREER LIBRARY   89

About the Author

Mike Martinez is a 10-year veteran of business journalism whose coverage of Wall Street has appeared in newspapers around the globe. He is a former editor at *Kiplinger's Personal Finance* and author of *Practical Tech for Your Business*. He is also the author of the *Vault Guide to Private Wealth Management* and co-author of *Vault Career Guide to Hedge Funds*.

Visit the Vault Finance Career Channel at **www.vault.com**/finance — with insider firm profiles, message boards, the Vault Consulting Job Board and more.

V\ULT CAREER LIBRARY

91